WITHDRAWN

Get **more** out of libraries

Please return or renew this item by the last date shown.

You can renew online at www.hants.gov.uk/library

Or by phoning   0300 555 1387

Hampshire
County Council

WIN

C016176028

D1429581

KELLY HOPPEN HOME

For Tash
with all
my love

jacqui
small

KELLY HOPPEN HOME

from concept to reality

TEXT BY HELEN CHISLETT • PHOTOGRAPHS BY VINCENT KNAPP

First published in 2007 by Jacqui Small,
7 Greenland Street, London NW1 0ND

Publisher Jacqui Small
Art Director Lawrence Morton
Project Editor Zia Mattocks
Production Peter Colley

ISBN: 978 1 903221 91 4

A catalogue record for this book is available
from the British Library.

10 9 8 7 6 5 4 3 2

Printed and bound in China

PAGE 1 *Detail of a dining table coated in textured plaster mixed with marble dust and mother-of-pearl natural pigment (see page 162 top), with vases by Anna Torfs.*
PAGES 2–3 *Detail of a bathroom cupboard with integral tungsten light and taps designed by Kelly Hoppen for Waterfront (see page 125 bottom).*
PAGE 4 *Kelly's kitchen with stainless-steel cooking hood positioned over the hob.*
PAGE 5 *Detail of a carved wooden screen, looking from the hall to the dining room with a chandelier by Mark Brazier-Jones (see page 31).*

FORE
WORD

Musing about the word 'home' and what it means to me, I found myself transported back to my grandparents' house just outside Cape Town. It was called Stone House and it enjoyed the best views in the locality, but it was also the most incredible family home. I left South Africa when I was two, but we went back to Stone House every Christmas and I absolutely loved it.

It may surprise you to know that it was very old-fashioned, with log fires and antique heirlooms. The first thing I would notice was the smell of coffee, because my grandmother stored it in a cedar chest in the hall. I can still visualize the bay seat in the drawing room where she would patiently teach me to crochet, sweets kept in big jars and Ella, the cook, baking delicious chocolate cakes. I remember the fabric combinations being extraordinary, too – suedes, leathers, chenilles and velvets, with buttoning on cushions – so that was clearly an influence.

My grandmother had the most exquisite hydrangea garden full of prize blooms. We used to pick them together and then go to a cupboard in the dining room where she kept china and glass collected from all over the world. Perhaps we would choose a Venetian glass vase or a porcelain one from France. Then I would help her to lay the table, because she knew I loved to do it. Everything in that cupboard was there to be used. She was never precious about what she had, knowing that if you save something for the right moment, that moment will never come. I never realized until much later in life how important Stone House was to me, because it was a safe haven where I could do no wrong in the eyes of the people who lived there.

In those days a home was created over years and years, layered with patience and love. Today we expect to make one instantly. One of the best things clients ever say to me is, 'You have created something for me that feels as though I have been here all my life,' and I think perhaps that ability goes directly back to my grandmother's house. It has never mattered to me that the houses I design draw praise for the way they look. What matters is that they feel like home to those who live there.

When you create a home, you create one to live in now – not tomorrow, next month, next year, but now. There is no better time than today. My hope is that, with this book, you, too, can transform your house into a home that feels as perfect to you as Stone House did to me all those years ago.

KELLY THE CLIENT

Like a lot of my clients, I was spurred to move because I had reached a different point in my life. What I wanted was a New York-style loft apartment. I walked in and knew instantly this was the most extraordinary space: it is enormous – 375 sq m / 4,035 sq ft – and once formed the major portion of a girls' school in south London. It lent itself perfectly to the idea of zoning, with one big room in which to place kitchen, living and dining areas. I could see immediately the structural changes I would make – knocking walls down, reconfiguring rooms – but every time

I went back, I changed my mind. The fact is that as a client you can afford that luxury; when you work for someone else, you can be strict.

I am spontaneous by nature, so I bought the apartment and then decided I hated it because it was so huge. For months I convinced myself I would do it up and sell it on, but slowly I came round to it. Now I absolutely adore it. The moral of that is to trust your first instincts; they often remain true, though it is difficult to remember that when you are elbow deep in builders' dust.

Interior designers with their own homes are like the cobbler with his shoes — we never give quite the same care and attention as we do when designing for someone else. I designed the whole of my apartment in an afternoon. I knew I wanted the grandest of bedrooms, bathrooms and dressing rooms. I knew I wanted a gallery-style hall where I could hang art. I knew I wanted a gym where the kitchen had originally been. I knew I wanted to create a snug in the little space above the living room, where I could watch television and hibernate in winter. And I knew I wanted a stunning roof terrace that would be a joy in summer. Happily, I got it all right, even though I did it in such a rush. The only flaw is that I should have allowed for a much bigger table in the kitchen, because kitchens are now where we all prefer to live and eat, rather than the dining room.

If I made one big mistake with this project, it was rushing it. I was renting a house while the work was being done and I should have rented for one more month. Even just a couple of late deliveries can cause problems, because certain people can't finish what they should be doing and then everyone starts falling behind. I had set a deadline for moving in, and in their attempt to make that happen some of the team were working round the clock.

In terms of decoration, I knew I wanted to do something very different here. The trick was to still keep the walls plain, either white or taupe, and to stain the original floorboards black. Then I could add infusions of colour through fabrics, rugs, flowers and photography. Because the main room is so enormous, it could have looked very boring – just one large space filled with furniture. I needed ways of introducing visual punctuation, so the hugeness of it was not overwhelming. The screen behind the staircase is a punctuation point, as is the Bubble chair suspended from the ceiling. For me, that chair really makes the room.

I also wanted to use furniture to make more of a statement. Whereas before I used to play with fabrics to create a visual shock – rich taffeta juxtaposed with slubby hemp, for example, or matt felt paired with shimmery silk – now I like to do a similar thing with the forms of furniture and objects. I love taking antique and vintage finds and placing them against the clean lines of stark contemporary pieces. You take what is safe and then add that twist to it. It rejuvenates both your home and you as a person.

I have also moved right away here from the perfection of the pure minimalist look. For example, my hi-fi speakers are suspended from the ceiling, not camouflaged away. I like the honesty of that. I also opted to use the original floorboards wherever possible, even though they were not in a great state. The dressing room is walk-in with open shelves — no cupboards — a decision that I not only enjoy visually, but that also saved me thousands of pounds.

The whole experience has given me even more insight into the pitfalls people face when designing their own homes. What I have learnt is that everybody likes too many different things. There are so many great products and ranges out there that it is easy to lose one's way — people think they can have it all. My job as a designer is to coax my clients — this way and that way — but often when people are left to their own devices, they pile it all in. You can love a million different styles, but the only way to get a look right is to edit down and down. This apartment is my ultimate dream, but with discipline and forethought you can create your own dream, too.

Kelly at home

THE CHALLENGE: To bring a Victorian school room into the twenty-first century, while retaining its inherent architectural features. To lose none of the wow factor of the double-height aspect, while also transforming it into a welcoming home.

THE SOLUTION: To stain original floorboards throughout, keep walls and fabrics neutral, then use a mix of contemporary and vintage furniture and lighting to add character and wit.

KEY CONSIDERATIONS

Imbuing such a vast space with a feeling of warmth and cosiness.

Zoning it effectively to make the space workable.

Making the most of original features, such as beams, floorboards and windows.

Reconfiguring the layout, in particular the location of the kitchen.

Finding pieces of furniture bold enough for the dimensions of the room.

Creating a neutral canvas.

Adding accents of colour and texture.

Replacing existing doors with super-tall contemporary ones.

Finding window treatments suitable for such huge expanses of glass.

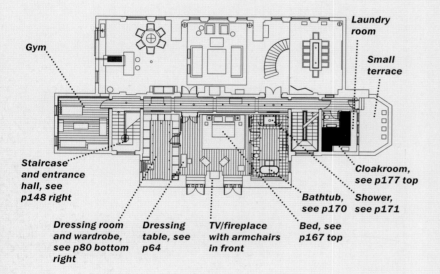

Gym

Laundry room

Small terrace

Staircase and entrance hall, see p148 right

Cloakroom, see p177 top

Dressing room and wardrobe, see p80 bottom right

Dressing table, see p64

TV/fireplace with armchairs in front

Bathtub, see p170

Shower, see p171

Bed, see p167 top

LEFT *The floor plan of the apartment showing the main open-plan living space above and, shaded below, the other key rooms: the master suite of bedroom, bathroom and dressing room; the hall; home gym; cloakroom; laundry and small terrace. The challenge was to unify the space rather than become overwhelmed by it.*
BELOW *A detailed view of the living space, which has been zoned into three distinct areas: kitchen and informal dining; seating; and formal dining. The position of the staircase, which separates living and dining areas, is a pivotal part of the visual punctuation.*

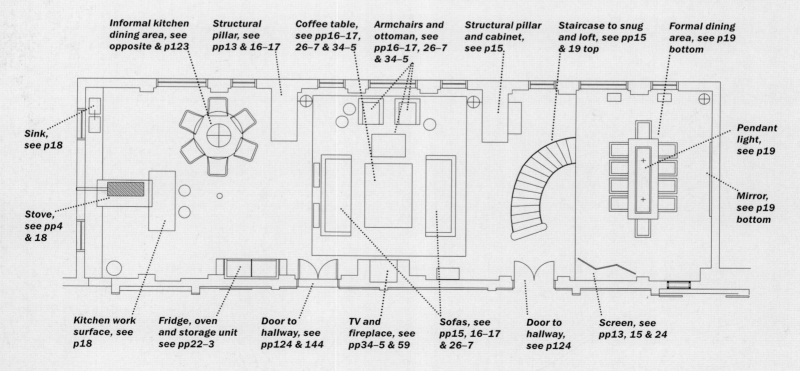

Informal kitchen dining area, see opposite & p123

Structural pillar, see pp13 & 16–17

Coffee table, see pp16–17, 26–7 & 34–5

Armchairs and ottoman, see pp16–17, 26–7 & 34–5

Structural pillar and cabinet, see p15

Staircase to snug and loft, see pp15 & 19 top

Formal dining area, see p19 bottom

Sink, see p18

Pendant light, see p19

Stove, see pp4 & 18

Mirror, see p19 bottom

Kitchen work surface, see p18

Fridge, oven and storage unit see pp22–3

Door to hallway, see pp124 & 144

TV and fireplace, see pp34–5 & 59

Sofas, see pp15, 16–17 & 26–7

Door to hallway, see p124

Screen, see pp13, 15 & 24

THIS PAGE *This informal dining area is at the kitchen end of the huge open-plan space. The dark wood of the table echoes the stained floorboards and makes a yin-yang contrast with low white leather chairs, both from Modénature. A pendant light of chainmail by Ochre hangs above.*

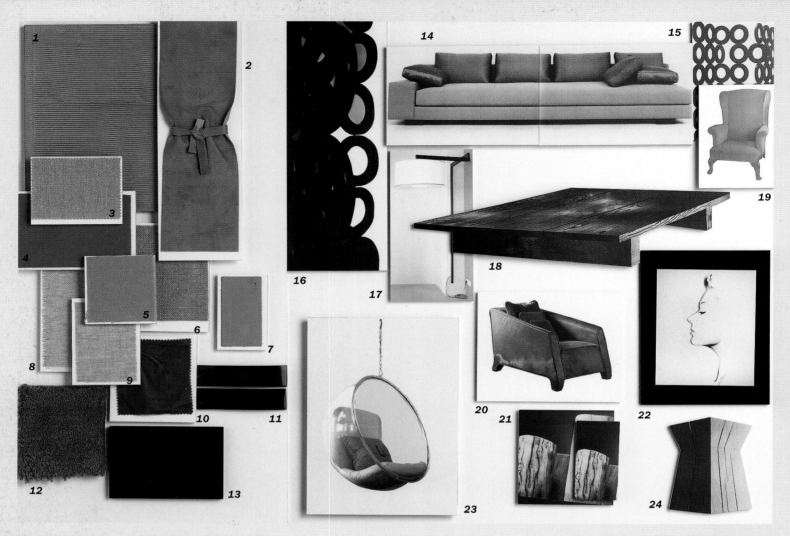

When you first find a home, you have to really imagine yourself living in it. Once I fell in love with this apartment, it took me barely any time to design it in my head and know exactly how I wanted to use the space. People associate my style with modernism and perfection, so at first glance this is a departure from my signature look. In many ways, though, it is classic Kelly – a yin-yang scheme of dark and pale, using a palette of neutral colours and contrasting textures. Where it differs from my previous home is that I have chosen to embrace the imperfections and irregularities of the period architecture, rather than try to impose something rigid upon it. Floorboards, windows and beams are left unchanged, but I have replaced the doors with dark stained modern ones that create panels of black against the white walls.

I did want to do something different here and I took inspiration from the vintage look that is so popular in the fashion world. The Perspex Bubble chair was really the making of the room for me – not only does it create a visual divide between the living area and kitchen, but it also adds such fun and character to the space. The wooden screen, my own design, achieves a similar effect at the other end of the room, partitioning off the formal dining area.

ROOM BOARD *What surprised me when I put the room board together was how little was actually on it – the room is huge, but the solution was to keep everything as simple as possible and to make full use of existing features.*

Starting with the fabrics on the left of the room board: linen is at the core of all my schemes and here it has been used on the sofas (6) and on the Roman blinds (9). Other blinds are made in loose-weave linen (8). Velvet is an excellent foil to linen in terms of texture and here I chose a yellow (5) for the armchair that is also a star piece and a more neutral shade for the side chairs (10). Leather (7) has been chosen for the ottoman base and cushions (4), while suede has been introduced onto cushions (2), complementing ones in linen (3). Slim horn buttons (11) have been used to embellish the cushions and add a note

of luxury. A silk rug (12) complements the stained wooden floor (13). The specialist plaster finish used around the fireplace (1) is the ideal backdrop for these rich textures.

To the right of the room board is the furniture selection, including the wooden screen I designed (15 and 16), Perspex Bubble chair by Eero Aarnio (23) and wrapped armchair (19), around which the rest of the scheme pivots. I needed bold overscaled pieces here, such as the generous 'Augustin' daybed by Christian Liaigre (14) – the 'Augustin' sofa was used in the final scheme (see opposite), coffee table (18) and lamp by India Mahdavi (17), but balanced these with scaled-down objects such as the stool of petrified wood by Bleu Nature (21) and the 'Nagato' stool by Christian Liaigre (24). Vintage-style armchairs (20) and artwork (22) add a further layer of visual interest.

THIS PAGE *A large open-plan space needs punctuation points – bold statement pieces to break up the big expanse of space. The suspended Perspex Bubble chair and wooden screen achieve that perfectly.*

RIGHT *A room as large as this demands large-scale pieces of furniture, such as the rustic-looking dark wood coffee table; this, together with the chunky 'Nagato' stools by Christian Liaigre, which I stained in a dark finish, connects visually to the old restored floorboards. The generous 'Augustin' sofas by Christian Liaigre came with me from my previous home, but I had them re-covered with suede on the outside and linen on the inside, transforming them into something entirely different. The armchairs are new, but by covering them in velvet that was not recommended for upholstery use, they have been given a vintage look. Using contrasting forms of furniture to create visual excitement is a natural progression for me, just as I have always combined fabrics of wildly different textures. The massive windows were a challenge in themselves: I wanted something that would unify them, allow light in by day, but be absolutely simple so as not to detract from the integrity of the architecture. The chainmail blinds are particularly effective at night when light shines down on them. The space is imposing enough to take them and the resulting effect is truly wonderful.*

KELLY'S INSIDER SECRETS

When you have a room as dramatic as this, you need a visual treatment that is quite toned down – rather than choosing something that will fight with the boldness of the existing space and architecture. I have unified the elements with a neutral palette.

In a period house it is easier to accept the quirkiness of age and architecture and go with it rather than try to impose perfection upon it. I kept the old cast-iron radiators, for example, rather than install underfloor heating – and my speakers are located on the ceiling for all to see. Why worry?

If you decide, as I did, to salvage original floorboards wherever possible, you must again accept that they will never be flawless. Renovating floorboards costs a great deal of time and money, but they are integral to the character of the space. If you want them dark like this, you must always stain rather than paint them.

When you are working with such a large space, the important thing is to keep it as simple as possible. When people first walk into my home, they do have that sense of 'wow' – but if they stopped to analyse what is going on, they would realize that my aim has been to allow the room to speak for itself rather than introduce elements that might fight within it and ultimately detract from its impact. The original floorboards have been stained black and the walls, woodwork and ceiling are painted just one colour, though I have also used specialist plaster effects for textural contrast. On this neutral palette I have used accents of colour, in particular the bright yellow of the wrapped armchair. It is surprising just how strong a statement this makes in such a vast room.

Scale is also key to the success of the scheme. Using fewer things, but of a larger scale, is far more effective in this loft-style apartment than filling it with a busy arrangement of objects and furniture. Size does not just apply to sofas and tables, but to the lighting and artwork I have chosen. To make large-scale objects appear even larger, I have juxtaposed them with small-scale items – such as the black-and-white photography in the formal dining room, which contrasts in size with the mirror, lamp and central light.

BELOW *The kitchen was originally located in the room I now use as my gym, but I wanted it in the main room because the kitchen is such an important part of the way we live today. Dark wood units are a visual anchor to the floor.*

OPPOSITE TOP LEFT AND RIGHT *The spiral stairs in the living area lead up to a platform, which I use as a snug. It is lovely to have an intimate space like this as a contrast to the grandeur of the main open-plan room. I had the staircase painted dark, so that its form stood out against the white walls. The bed base, vintage chair, 'Flibuste' pedestal tables by Christian Liaigre and lamp base by Kevin Reilly all tie in.*

OPPOSITE BELOW *The formal dining area is at the opposite end of the room to the kitchen. The ceiling is lower and I have accentuated this with a custom-made tasselled light made of linen and silk by Mat & Jewski. Textural contrast is further provided with the zebra skin and imposing carver chairs in faux crocodile. The giant Anglepoise lamp adds a witty touch and is in scale with the room's proportions.*

THE DESIGN PROCESS

Your home is your life, so respect that and give it the thought it deserves. It does not matter whether you are on the first rung of the property ladder with a one-bedroom flat to decorate or whether you have millions to spend creating your dream house from scratch. The properties shown here may be at the latter end of the scale, but the same rules apply and are accessible to everyone, no matter how big or small their home.

The starting point

You may already have a vision of your dream home, but first you need to spend time analysing what it is that you really want.

You may not be able to afford an interior designer, but there is no reason why you cannot be your own. Part of the challenge of working as a professional designer is trying to get into the client's head – before you can hope to come up with a design they will passionately want, you first have to understand how they live, what they love and what they most desire from their home. When you are your own client, you are already halfway there.

If you mentally step into the role of interior designer, you are more likely to stay focused on what the priorities are and what the budget will allow. It really does help the creative process if you can be strict with yourself. Designing a house is like getting dressed in the morning – you may have a lot of different styles in your wardrobe, but you wouldn't try to wear everything at once.

WRITE YOURSELF A BRIEF

Designing a home can be a confusing business and it is inevitable that at some point you will find it hard to see the wood for the trees. Begin by writing yourself a brief as if you were a client commissioning a designer; not only will this focus your mind on the priorities of what you wish to achieve, it will also be a useful reminder in the months to come – a way of staying in touch with your original vision. You don't have to make the brief complicated, but it must be written down, not just carried in your head.

RIGHT *In my own home I wanted a kitchen that would reflect the character of the main living space. Rather than opt for conventional kitchen units, I chose to integrate the Sub Zero fridge and oven into a bold architectural cupboard made of wenge to echo the dark stained floorboards. To the right of this is a striking piece of photographic artwork by Flip Schulke.*

Buy a large notebook
in which to write lists
and make notes.

As any designer will tell you, the first hurdle when meeting with a new client is not just assessing what they want from their home, but discovering what they need. It is not enough for a home to look spectacular; it has to work for whoever lives there on all levels.

I always begin by presenting a new client with a questionnaire that runs over many tens of pages. I require a great deal of detail. Which side of the bed do they sleep on? How important is exercise to them? How much television do they watch? Which cooking method do they most employ? It is important they understand that if they want a home custom-made for them, it is crucial that I examine their lives in depth. There would be no point commissioning

a couture gown if you were not prepared to have all your measurements taken. A home costs a great deal more than a piece of couture ever will, so it stands to reason it is even more essential to think long and deep about what you want from it.

When you are designing for yourself, you need to look beyond the fabrics you love or the furniture you are saving for and think first about the function you require from the space. You also need to be 100 per cent honest. You might fantasize about metamorphosing into a domestic goddess who spends hours in the kitchen baking cakes, but if the truth is that you will dash in, grab something out of the fridge and dash out again, then the priority is a large fridge, not a state-of-the-art

OPPOSITE *In my apartment the staircase is a visual divide between dining and living spaces. The screen makes the dining room even more secluded, and introduces a horizontal line to balance the vertical of the stairs.*

stove. You might think how fabulous it would be to create a drop-dead dining room for lavish dinner parties, but if you are more likely to enjoy informal suppers in the kitchen, then you need a kitchen that allows you to do just that. With each room you design, begin by writing down all the activities you and your family might pursue there – not just the obvious, but the ones that are quirky to you.

Unless you are designing just for yourself, you will also need to consider other people's desires. You want everyone to be happy in this house when it is finished. Men are generally less demanding – in my experience they list ten things they want, whereas women list fifty. If you want a contented life, give in on the ten. Children, too, need to have their say – I find many of my clients' children have very specific ideas about what they would like from their bedrooms, bathrooms or playrooms – the more ownership of a space a family has, the more likely they are to help maintain it.

This stage is important whether you are designing a house from plan up or redesigning a home where you have lived for many years. The first gives you more flexibility and opportunities, but that in itself can become bewildering: it makes it even more crucial to know where you are heading. The second scenario presents different problems – you need the ability to step outside of what has become familiar and comforting and to look for new solutions to a changing life. The self-analysis needed to kick-start the design process can be a little uncomfortable – it is all too easy to throw yourself into choosing colours or textures – but you must complete this stage if the rest of the project is going to run smoothly.

Once you have listed all your wants and needs, prioritize them – the must-haves to the would-likes. Now you are on the way to being your own interior designer.

QUESTIONNAIRE

Begin by asking yourself the following questions:

Which activities will take place in each room?

At which time of day are you most likely to use certain rooms?

What is each room adjacent to and how will you create a sense of flow?

Are you going to keep existing architectural features?

What are the plus/minus points of each room?

How much natural light is available and how is this likely to change through the seasons?

What do windows look out on and how can you capitalize on this?

Do you like to dine formally or informally?

Do you prefer to bathe or shower?

Do you need a proper cook's kitchen with space for all manner of utensils and equipment?

Is there space for a dressing room or do you need plenty of clothes storage in the bedroom?

Do you need to design better storage so possessions don't overwhelm you?

Which existing furniture/accessories are still to be used?

How are you going to link the inside to the outside?

Spatial planning

Now is the time to consider all the design possibilities of the space you have available.

There is a lot written in books such as these about the need to work from a flat plan when assessing space. The problem is that most people find it extremely hard to visualize something in 3-D when looking at a plan in 2-D. That is why in my company we present clients with elevations, rather than flat plans, when showing how a home will look. Elevations are costly, though – instead, you could use chalk or masking tape to indicate where furniture might be placed, or to mark how high something is against a wall. Some people have the gift of visualizing what the end result will be, while others really struggle. If you are in the latter camp, it might actually save you money to have elevations drawn up, as mistakes can be so expensive. If you do go down this route, you need one for every wall. They will help you to see where wall lights should be positioned or whether the dining chairs you have chosen are the correct height for the table you plan to use.

PLANS, PLANS AND MORE PLANS

If you are going to make structural changes that require plans to be drawn up, do make sure you number and date each set. It is all too easy for confusion to set in if your building team are working to slightly varying plans. Remember that everyone involved needs copies of the latest ones, so it is your responsibility to circulate them to plumbers, electricians, carpenters and so forth. It might sound obvious, but you also have to make sure you use the same scale throughout – each piece of furniture, for example, has to be scaled down using the same calculation as for the floor plan. If you are a mathematical dunce, enlist the help of someone who understands the difference between a scale of 1:20 and one of 1:50.

THIS PAGE *A bird's-eye view of my apartment showing the huge living area and the kitchen beyond. I wanted a sense of flow between each zone, but I used features such as the retro Bubble chair to mark out invisible boundaries (see pages 12–19 for more detail).*

RIGHT An imaginative approach was needed when it came to this Arts & Crafts home, because the fireplace is off-centre, meaning the living room lacks symmetry. Rather than fight with the proportions, I simply moved the seating area forward and lined up the sofa with the fireplace. To create a sense of balance, I then lined up the coffee table with three uniform pots. The floor plan below shows how this enabled me to impose a feeling of symmetry through the furniture layout.

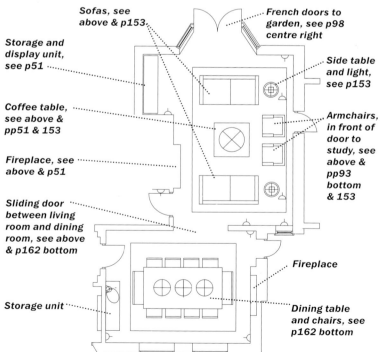

Sofas, see above & p153

French doors to garden, see p98 centre right

Storage and display unit, see p51

Side table and light, see p153

Coffee table, see above & pp51 & 153

Armchairs, in front of door to study, see above & pp93 bottom & 153

Fireplace, see above & p51

Sliding door between living room and dining room, see above & p162 bottom

Fireplace

Storage unit

Dining table and chairs, see p162 bottom

The whole point of spatial planning is to try to work out whether your original list of priorities for a room can be accommodated in the space provided. There might have to be compromises made, but don't despair. Sometimes compromises can inspire new creative solutions, such as putting a home-study area in the space under the stairs rather than in the living room, or situating a laundry area in the bathroom rather than in the kitchen.

Look at the space in the property as one fluid whole, rather than being constrained by existing partition walls. You might well be able to reconfigure it to suit your needs simply by knocking through two rooms or creating an L-shape with three. Don't allow yourself to become entrenched in the question of whether whatever you would like to do to the property will add or subtract value. You have to design for yourself and the way you live, not with a view to how much a house will be worth five years down the line. It is also important that you don't consider too many other opinions – everyone will have their own ideas as to how the space should be best used. Behave as an interior designer would – look for the best spatial solution for the required functions of the room.

If you are designing a room from scratch, you should also ask your lighting consultant or electrician to draw up an electrical plan. This will show where every socket and light switch is going.

ABOVE The staircase in this apartment is so sculptural and beautiful that I wanted a way of integrating it into the dining room, so it could be enjoyed as a focal point. These French-style panelled glass doors pivot, rather than open in a conventional manner, so when opened they extend the dining room into the hall. Not only does this have the effect of borrowing views and light from one room into the other, it is also a visually interesting way of treating doors in halls. The floor plan (right) shows clearly the relationship between the dining room and stairs.

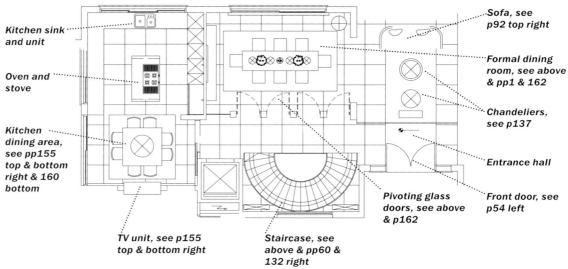

Kitchen sink and unit

Oven and stove

Kitchen dining area, see pp155 top & bottom right & 160 bottom

TV unit, see p155 top & bottom right

Staircase, see above & pp60 & 132 right

Pivoting glass doors, see above & p162

Sofa, see p92 top right

Formal dining room, see above & pp1 & 162

Chandeliers, see p137

Entrance hall

Front door, see p54 left

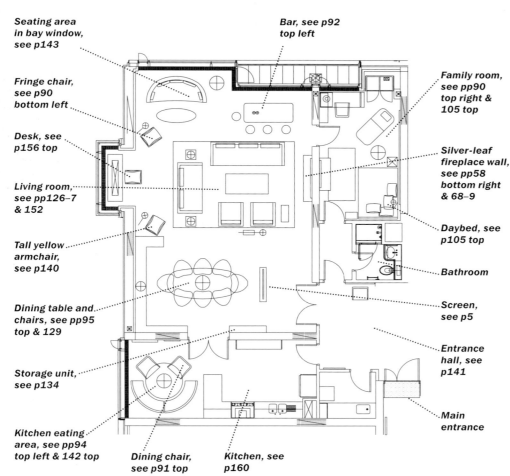

Seating area
in bay window,
see p143

Bar, see p92
top left

Fringe chair,
see p90
bottom left

Family room,
see pp90
top right &
105 top

Desk, see
p156 top

Silver-leaf
fireplace wall,
see pp58
bottom right
& 68–9

Living room,
see pp126–7
& 152

Daybed, see
p105 top

Tall yellow
armchair,
see p140

Bathroom

Dining table and
chairs, see pp95
top & 129

Screen,
see p5

Storage unit,
see p134

Entrance
hall, see
p141

Kitchen eating
area, see pp94
top left & 142 top

Main
entrance

Dining chair,
see p91 top

Kitchen, see
p160

*THIS PAGE AND OPPOSITE This city apartment is a
good example of one-space living. The functions
of this room include a living space with home
cinema, dining area, study and bar. Each zone
had to have its own identity as well as work from
a functional point of view. The artwork (top left)
was drawn up to show the clients what I
envisioned for the space, including the faux
fireplace, wall-mounted plasma screen, bar
area and two separate seating areas. Very little
changed from the concept to the reality, except
for the location of the screen, which was
positioned in front of the dining table in order
to separate it visually from the main door to
the room. The textured walls, patterned rug
by Am Collections and the furniture shapes by
Christian Liaigre have remained constant (see
room board on pages 38–9). The flat plan (left)
shows the furniture layout, with the bar and
additional seating area at one end adjacent*

to the family room; the main seating area in front of the fireplace; the dining area and screen; and beyond this the kitchen with family dining space. Doors to each area open from a relatively small hall, meaning space has been maximized to the full. The photograph (above) shows the finished effect looking in the opposite direction from the artwork, from the main seating area to the dining area. Lighting has been used to delineate and enhance each area (see pages 126–9 for more on this), while a wealth of texture, from the silver leaf on the walls to the crystal of the Mark Brazier-Jones chandelier, has been used to bring in warmth and personality. The client's incredible collection of art, including this photographic piece by Vanessa Beecroft, has been displayed to great effect. It is a successful conclusion to a challenge that meant manipulating space to the best advantage, while creating something visually arresting.

Do not cut corners on light sockets; they are not easy to add in once the decoration is complete. Generally speaking, people need a lot more sockets in a room than they think they will. You might also need sockets in the floor for reading lamps behind sofas – a trailing wire is not only dangerous but unsightly. You have to be very sure before installing floor sockets, as they do dictate the furniture layout of a room and floorboards or carpet have to be cut to accommodate them.

Pay attention to details. If you plan built-in cupboards, how much space do the doors need to open properly? If you are using freestanding radiators, you cannot place good furniture in front of them so they will need to be attractive. If you are planning to buy some really big pieces of furniture, have you checked not only that they will fit in the room, but that they will get through the front door? By the time you have finished your assessment, you should be confident about what it will be possible to achieve in the room, how it can be achieved and how much it will cost.

FIRST THINGS FIRST

Be honest about whether there are improvements to be made to what I call the 'boring essentials' – heating, electrics, plumbing and so forth. Also assure yourself there are no underlying structural problems to deal with at this stage. If this is a new home for you, pay attention to what the surveyor has told you. It might be tempting to get straight in there and begin redecorating, but if the property is not sound and well maintained, you will regret your haste. It is undeniably irritating to see a huge chunk of your budget disappear on things that can't be enjoyed visually, but there is nothing to be gained by storing up problems for the future. So bite the bullet and put these things to rights.

Plumbing and electrics are the 'underwear' of a room – you might not be able to see them, but without them you would be only half dressed. There is nothing worse than sharing your home with builders, so the sensible thing to do is to get all this over with at the very beginning and then hopefully you won't have to ask them back again. If you are having a home-security system installed, now is the time to do it – not when the flooring is down and the wallpaper is up. The same goes for integrated audiovisual systems, which allow you to enjoy music wherever you may be in the house.

However, the most crucial piece of 'underwear' is lighting. The more circuits you have in a room, the more you can vary the effect of different light sources, such as recessed lights, table lamps, uplighters, wall sconces and so forth. If you can afford it, engage a lighting consultant. Once you have worked with one, you will be educated about lighting and whenever you decorate a home in the future you will find it is second nature to you. Don't be scared of the cost – most are the equivalent of a long weekend away, and lighting really is something you will never regret spending your money on. The fact is that a fairly modest room will look spectacular when lit well, whereas a beautifully decorated one will look flat and uninteresting if lit badly.

Architectural considerations

To design well, you have to be sympathetic to the architectural style and age of the building itself.

Doors, windows, staircases and so forth form the permanent architecture of the room. If you are redecorating an existing property, you might well decide they are too expensive to change. However, if you are designing from the ground up, you need to spend time making sure you get these important elements right.

Let us look first at the architecture in an existing property. Don't feel you have to keep period features for the sake of it. If a building is listed, you probably have no choice, but there is no rule that says all fireplaces, picture rails or dados are unquestionably a good thing. Ornamental ceiling cornices can accommodate really contemporary schemes, so they are usually best kept. I like to draw the eye upwards in a room, so the more beautiful the ceiling, the better. Picture rails, dados and skirtings, however, often have the effect of shortening the dimensions of a room by accentuating the horizontal. If you remove them, you make the room appear taller. You also create huge planes on which to play with colour and texture.

When dealing with period architectural features, my own tendency is to keep them and create really contemporary effects around them. It is all a question of balance. Get rid of fireplaces at your peril – you might think you don't want one, but absolutely nothing makes a room feel more wonderful than an old-fashioned fire. If the design is mediocre, then replace it with a contemporary one rather than boarding it up for ever.

Staircases are often too expensive to change completely, but if you have one that is not listed there are ways to give it a whole new lease of life, from staining or painting wood to replacing balustrades or adding stair rods.

Adding or removing windows is costly, and you can usually improve on window proportions instead by being clever with curtains and blinds. You can, however, replace doors relatively easily. I deal with doors in more detail on pages 54–7, but would emphasize here that you should have the tallest, most imposing doors possible – they sweep the eye upwards and create a strong signature look.

OPPOSITE *Marvellous contemporary interiors can be created in buildings of age and pedigree. This Georgian orangery has been converted into a chic home office and library, furnished with a comfortable sofa and ottomans, along with 'Barbuda' chairs, bronze pedestal table and 'Pastora' lights by Christian Liaigre. The specially commissioned staircase, double-height shelves and floor-to-ceiling blinds all sweep the eye upwards.*

If you are building from scratch, you are in the fortunate position of being able to make every design choice right down to the height of the skirting board or the width of a window. Take your time. These are the sorts of choices that people often pay little heed to, thinking them relatively unimportant. In fact, they are the bone structure of a room, a chance to create a space that is beautifully in proportion before you even begin to decorate. Clients are often amazed at the detail I go into when designing skirting boards, for example – it is not unusual for me to incorporate lighting or combine materials such as mirror, beading and glass. I like to go to town on skirtings, precisely because they are often ignored. At other times I prefer to follow the purist line and have no skirting at all, just a clean edge from floor to wall. The important thing is to really think about what you want, not just to opt for the standard treatment simply because it falls within the builder's comfort zone.

Finally, remember that internal architecture can be used to improve the proportions of a room. Rooms are essentially grid systems on which you can play with the vertical and horizontal. As I have already mentioned, if you want to make a room appear taller, then remove picture rails and skirting boards, which shorten a wall, and replace standard doors with extra-tall ones. If you want to make it appear wider, then skirtings, dados and picture rails will all help to do this. The one golden rule I would always apply is to paint all the internal architecture, including windows, the same colour as the walls. That way, the eye can flow smoothly around the space and the room automatically appears larger.

RIGHT *In a big space, such as my apartment, the key is to choose furniture and furnishings of a suitably large scale, so the space doesn't feel overwhelming (see page 14). In addition to scaling up the internal architecture, such as the double-height doors, I chose furniture and art that made a statement, such as the pieces by Kimiko Yoshida (left) and Gene Kornman (right). In a room this high, it is easy to stress the vertical, particularly with the staircase leading up to the snug, but this is balanced by the strong horizontal lines of the Christian Liaigre 'Augustin' sofas, the coffee table and the screen. There is no more furniture here than in a conventionally sized living room, but it has all been selected for its form, scale and character.*

Design considerations

The time has come to let your imagination flow and to begin collating the bones of your scheme.

Of course, you are longing to get to the next stage and start thinking about how your home will look when it is finished. Style influences come from all over the place – travel, restaurants, fashion, history, nature and iconic people, to name but a few. Many people begin to collect pictures and cuttings from magazines and other visual reminders long before they even find the home they want to buy. I always find it a great help when clients start emptying onto my desk fabric swatches, paint charts, postcards and photographs that they have gathered over the months. The problem is that often we find too much that we like – you have to play around with all these fragments of visual memory until you begin to feel in which direction you should be going.

It is essential to make room boards for each space you are designing. These can combine both the visual inspiration you have collected and particular samples of fabric, flooring, furniture and so on. I always begin with fabrics – lots of them. By laying down many different ones, I begin to get a feel for the room. It is the point at which I really start to visualize what I am going to do. At this stage I don't know what any of the fabrics will be for – in fact, I positively avoid thinking about that; I use them initially to build up the tonal palette and to create a certain mood. People can get fixated on fabrics; they fall in love with one and become determined to use it. That, to me, is the wrong approach because there is a danger of getting stuck at that point. Fabrics should flow.

Room boards also mean doing a lot of research and legwork. You might have decided, for example, on a limestone floor in

TOP RIGHT *A full-length mirror with a leather-covered frame has been juxtaposed with a dark wood dressing table, creating a vignette in this chalet bedroom. The stool seat is upholstered in leather and the lampshade, from Porta Romana, is made of silk.*

BOTTOM RIGHT *Flooring is an expensive and permanent design decision. Here a runner of yin polished limestone has been inset into the yang of black stained oak floorboards.*

OPPOSITE TOP *When choosing materials for your home, think about the character intrinsic to each one. Here pebble resin from Byrock has been used to provide textural contrast against the smooth ceramic of the basin.*

OPPOSITE BOTTOM *The jewel-like red velvet sofa is enhanced by the gold wax plaster wall effect. The sculptural bronze pedestal table by Christian Liaigre is positioned to play against the metal grid of the underfloor heating.*

the bathroom. But which colour of limestone? Where from? How much? You may have to order six or seven samples before deciding which one to add to the board. And, of course, the same goes for every other design ingredient you plan to introduce, from the colour and finish of paint to the dimensions of a sofa. You can't rush this process. If the project is going to run successfully, you need to have made 90 per cent of your design decisions before the builders arrive. Everyone changes their mind endlessly and you will be no different. What matters is that you change your mind while you still can.

If I have one criticism when I see other people's room boards, it is that often they are not detailed enough. It is not just a matter of showing your chosen flooring, paint colours, window treatments and furniture. You need to include every fabric and textural element right down to the buttons on the cushions or the type of art you plan to hang. This is also the place to make decisions on door furniture, plasma screens, taps, light switches – every single design ingredient you are planning to introduce into the scheme. You also need to photograph furniture and other objects that you are planning on integrating into the new scheme. Again, this is the time for total honesty: are they helping or hindering your ideas? This may be the moment when you have to let some things go, either for ever or into storage. Lay the room boards out in as clear and precise a way as you are able. They may be 'only for you', but they are the blueprint for the room and, as such, they are of great significance.

ORDER OF CONSIDERATION

When designing a room, I consider elements in this order:

Fabrics They create a tonal palette from which to work and allow me to begin playing with textural contrast.

Furniture It is form and texture that most interest me at the design stage, rather than function.

Details Inlays on furniture, buttoning on cushions, materials for door panels – all opportunities to introduce layers of texture.

Star pieces The big statements, whether it is artwork, focal pieces of furniture or fabulous collections.

Window treatments These could be anything from simple shutters to glamorous curtains.

Floors and walls The big planes of the room – the canvas on which everything else plays.

Lighting An essential element in any room, but one that can't be planned until every design decision has been made.

KELLY SAYS

Every room board that I do contains at least one linen – it seems to anchor everything else in place.

ROOM BOARD *This is the room board shown for the apartment featured in Case Study 6: In The Mood – Lighting (see pages 126–9) and Case Study 8: In the Mood – Art (see pages 140–3). A flat plan and artist's interpretation of the living room of the apartment are also shown on page 30.*

The brief was to create a multifunctional space within a purpose-built apartment, with living area, home cinema, bar, study corner and dining area within one room. Not only did it have to work from a practical point of view, but each space also had to have its own character, while still allowing the eye to flow smoothly from zone to zone.

Beginning with the fabrics to the left of the board, I chose a rich dark velvet (5) for one sofa and a paler herringbone (6) for another. These were echoed in the cushions (2 and 3). A complementary pigskin suede was chosen for additional cushions (11), banded in silk (8). Curtains (14) are made of loose-weave linen. Leather was also an important element, used in a light shade on armchairs (12) and in a darker faux-crocodile version for the seats of the bar stools (9) and on the ottoman I designed (21). Linen lampshades (4) add a further note of elegance. The backdrop for these wonderful textures is the silver-finish wallpaper (1) and the linen-hued paint (10). A stone finish on the fireplace (13) and wood finishes on the floorboards, doors, joinery and shelving (15) are also at the core of the scheme.

To the right of the board are the key pieces of furniture. Seating is a confident mix of forms, such as the curved sofa from Interior Craft (28), the bar stools by India Mahdavi (29) and the tall armchair (24). The latter is covered in yellow velvet (7), the same as that used in my own apartment (see pages 14, 24 and 89). These statement pieces are juxtaposed with comfortable seating in the form of Christian Liaigre's 'Mousson' sofas and armchairs (17 and 19) and a generously sized wood coffee table, 'Toja', also by Christian Liaigre (20). A chainmail fringe is an unusual addition to one of my own armchair designs (26). The study area is furnished with a dark wood desk (27) and an office chair upholstered in leather from Donghia (30). Stools of aged wood from Interior Craft (23) and petrified wood from Bleu Nature (25) add further texture. Table lamps by Mathieu Lustrerie (18) and Interior Craft (22) are on a separate lighting circuit, while a floor lamp (31) adds drama. The clients' own collection of artwork (16), including pieces by Jean Baptiste Huynh, is also central to the scheme.

16

17

18

19

20

21

22

23

24

25

26

27

28

29

30

31

FROM CONCEPT TO REALITY

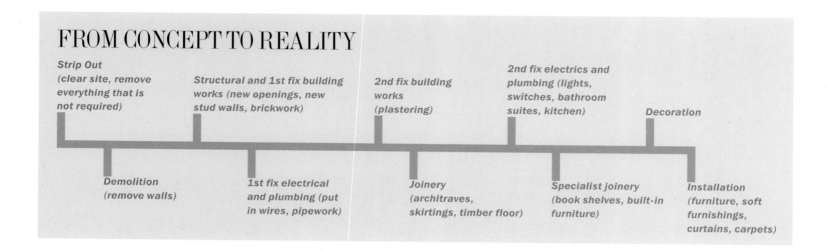

Strip Out (clear site, remove everything that is not required)

Demolition (remove walls)

Structural and 1st fix building works (new openings, new stud walls, brickwork)

1st fix electrical and plumbing (put in wires, pipework)

2nd fix building works (plastering)

Joinery (architraves, skirtings, timber floor)

2nd fix electrics and plumbing (lights, switches, bathroom suites, kitchen)

Specialist joinery (book shelves, built-in furniture)

Decoration

Installation (furniture, soft furnishings, curtains, carpets)

BUDGET

One of the most depressing things to happen when designing a home is that you simply run out of money. It is also frighteningly easy to do.

Take it from me, the first thing to remember is that you will always need more money than you think you will. Do your sums and then add on at least another 20 per cent contingency fund. This should cover all those unexpected scenarios, from builders unearthing some structural fault that has to be dealt with to a late delivery that forces you to look elsewhere for certain goods.

Secondly, don't imagine that it is enough to get the core done – lighting, flooring, sanitaryware and so on – and that it won't matter if you have to wait months, even years, for the furniture, fabrics, art or accessories you want. You will be miserable living in a half-decorated house. You must go back to your room board and compromise. There is no shame in this. As an interior designer, I help clients to compromise all the time in order to bring a job in within budget. What good would it be to them if I refused to compromise and they had to move into a house with no sofas, lamps or door furniture? The fact is, there are wonderful affordable ranges available. If you have set your heart on one special item, then treat yourself, but only if you have found ways to make savings elsewhere.

Thirdly, don't make false economies. I mentioned in 'Kelly The Client' (pages 8–11) the mistake I made in not renting for one more month while my own home was finished – it proved to be a false economy. In my experience, there is no such thing as a bargain, either. Life seems to decree that 'bargains' always come with hidden costs – basins that require non-standard taps, for example, or furniture that has to be winched into a property by crane because it won't fit through the door and up the stairs. It has also become fashionable to look for bargains online. In theory, this is fine, but are you confident that you will have the same consumer protection as you would from a shop if something substandard arrives? If not, your 'cheap' buy could turn out to be a disaster.

Finally, although you must be honest about how expensive doing up your home will be and know you have the funds to cover it, you might have a few months – depending on the size of the project – in which to pay all the money. As long as you have the bulk of it upfront and know when the rest will materialize, you can spread the cost over a given length of time. This can sweeten the pill if costs do start to spiral.

BE YOUR OWN PROJECT MANAGER

One benefit of hiring a professional interior designer is that he or she takes the stress of running the project off your hands. It is not up to you to waste hours waiting for plumbers to arrive or kitchens to be delivered. In my company we allocate an average of eight people to each job we do, so that we can cover absolutely everything that needs to be thought about.

If you are going to be your own interior designer, you will also need to be your own project manager. This means you are going to have to give a lot of time to making sure things run smoothly – time that you might usually use for working, socializing, exercising, shopping and all manner of other things. In other words, be prepared for the fact that your life will be turned upside down while all this is going on.

There is a law – let us call it Kelly's Law – that decrees that if you take your eye off the ball for a moment, a decision will be made on site that makes your stomach flip over when you see the result. A beautifully distressed original door will be gloss-painted. The plaster you wanted rough and rustic will be super-smooth. The door you wanted hung left to right will be hung right to left, so it knocks against a piece of furniture when opened. Some of these mistakes might be easy to rectify, but some could be irreversible – they will all cost you money to put right.

Draw up a schedule of work in the most minute detail you can. To do this you will first have to list all the individual jobs within the project. It might help to work backwards – the final job is usually putting down the flooring, but even this has implications. If it is carpet, you will probably lay it once the skirtings are in place. If it is a hard floor, you might want the skirtings to be positioned afterwards for a really neat finish. If, like me, you don't want skirtings at all, then how are you going to make a neat join between floor and wall? There are questions like this to answer at every single step of the way.

Work out how much time must be allowed for each stage – build in several days' grace between one team finishing and another starting. Can you rotate people around the house from room to room, or will this create more problems than it solves? It is crucial that your various teams can work when they expect to, otherwise – horror of horrors – they might disappear off to another job.

Allow plenty of time to find your dream team of builders, electricians, plumbers and so forth. Word of mouth is the best recommendation, but if you come across someone who looks promising, check them out by asking to visit properties where they have worked and to talk direct to past clients. Always ask more than one person to tender for a job. Sealed bids ensure really competitive quotes, but don't necessarily hire the cheapest. Once you have made your choice, check that they can fit into the proposed time scale.

Double check all delivery times. How confident are you in your suppliers? What are you going to do if key items do not arrive when they should? Who is going to be on site when deliveries arrive and who is going to check their quality? If you take delivery of an item too early, it can cause nearly as many problems as one arriving late. Not only do you have to find somewhere to store it, but the chances are that you will keep it protected in all its packaging. If you unpack it six weeks later and find a fault, you have not only weakened your right to return shoddy goods, but you will now have to wait days or weeks for a replacement to be found.

Communicate. Photocopy your schedule of works and distribute it to all involved parties, so they can understand why it is crucial for them to fit into a certain time schedule. If they can't, you need to know about it now.

Pay on time but don't hand over all the money until a task is finished. Financial incentive is the best carrot there is.

Visit the site daily. If you don't, not only might you not be on hand when key decisions have to be made, but you won't be aware if someone is falling behind.

Keep your cool. It is not in your interests to fall out with the very people you are relying on – you need all your negotiation skills.

Say thank you. Once your dream home is complete, invite all those involved to come back and see the finished space for themselves – it gives everyone a boost to know how successful a project has been. It also makes it far more likely they will offer you some sort of customer care should anything go wrong in the first few months.

KELLY SAYS

Buy folders and have one for every room you are designing. Use them to keep quotations, samples, delivery dates and other paperwork.

A dream come true

THE CHALLENGE: To take a client's ultimate requirements for her absolute dream home and make sure it became reality, from large-scale vision to the tiniest detail.

THE SOLUTION: To allow the imagination to soar, knowing that anything is, in fact, possible. To encourage the client to communicate all her ideas and inspirations.

There are landmark projects in every designer's career, and for me the opportunity to create this home was one in a million. It is a house that was built from the ground up and I was involved in every stage of its development, working in tandem with the wonderful architect Rebecca Rasmussen. The clients had brought up their family in a house built on the same site, but when the children had grown up and left home, they decided to knock it down and create the house they had always dreamt of – inch by inch and brick by brick.

What made it so special for me was the client's determination to be involved at every step of the way. She wanted every nail and screw to be just right, and that sort of dedication shows. You cannot have a better combination than a client with such love and care for what she is doing, assisted by an architect and designer who share the same sensibilities. It is a winning force.

BELOW *One of the joys of creating a home from scratch is that you can ensure there are vistas from every room. The view here is looking from the family living room through the connecting corridor to the formal dining room. Each one of the reclaimed floorboards was chosen by hand.*

OPPOSITE TOP *The centrepiece of the dining room is a Linley table, inlaid with mother-of-pearl, which was specially commissioned for the space. Curtains of silk and satin fall in cascades to the floor.*

OPPOSITE BOTTOM *The floors and window treatments in the living room echo those in the dining room, creating a sense of flow – something that is important in such a large house. Symmetry and balance are also key to the calm and serenity of the space.*

KEY CONSIDERATIONS

Creating a new family home on the same site as the clients' existing family house.

Taking the blueprint for such a large house and making sure it flowed effortlessly from room to room.

Communicating continuously with the client to take all her ideas on board.

Thinking about both the big picture – the layout – and the tiniest decorative details.

Allowing enough time, not only at the planning stage but for all the specially commissioned items.

Integrating existing pieces of furniture and objects into the new scheme and updating them where necessary.

Making sure that for all its space and luxurious touches, the house still felt like a cosy family home.

It is an enormous house – 2,415 sq m / 26,000 sq ft – but the joy of designing an interior from the plans up is that anything is possible because anything can be changed. Once the client had shown me her collection of magazine cuttings and explained the things that were most important to her, I could simply let my imagination fly. Rebecca was extraordinary to work with and we both took such care over the planning of it that, by the time it was built, it was absolutely perfect.

The client had a great sense of the East, loved the Art Deco period and owned a lot of traditional furniture, too, so the challenge from a design point of view was making sure that this cross-reference of styles all worked well together. We were also fortunate enough to be able to commission many special pieces of furniture for the house, even locating a Japanese craft consortium, Miya Shoji, that could make traditional shoji panels.

The clients own a stud farm and I wanted to make a reference to this within the house, hence the inspiration for the double-height library with its stitched-leather floor and chimney breast (see pages 45–6). It is an extraordinarily striking room, and it is wonderful to see what can happen when you aim to make dreams come true. One of my best moments was inviting these clients back into their home and seeing their joy at what, together, we had created.

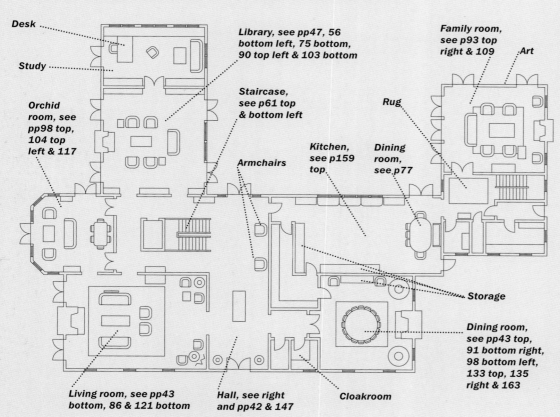

Desk

Study

Orchid room, see pp98 top, 104 top left & 117

Library, see pp47, 56 bottom left, 75 bottom, 90 top left & 103 bottom

Staircase, see p61 top & bottom left

Armchairs

Kitchen, see p159 top

Dining room, see p77

Family room, see p93 top right & 109

Art

Rug

Storage

Dining room, see pp43 top, 91 bottom right, 98 bottom left, 133 top, 135 right & 163

Living room, see pp43 bottom, 86 & 121 bottom

Hall, see right and pp42 & 147

Cloakroom

ABOVE *The floor plan shows the ground floor of the house, with the hall as the spine from which other key rooms, such as the living room and dining room, radiate. The staircase at the far end of the hall provides a natural divide between the kitchen and family areas and the more formal library.*

RIGHT *The entrance hall sets the signature for the rest of the house, with extra-wide reclaimed floorboards, silk carpet and specialist plaster finish. The crushed-velvet chair is placed here as a piece of sculpture rather than furniture; its scale and form balance that of the antique figures by the door. The door to the left leads to the dining room and the one to the right to the living room, creating views from one to the other (see page 42).*

OPPOSITE TOP *The finished room is a triumph, complete with double-height leather chimney breast and stitched-leather floor. Bill Amberg flew in personally to stitch the leather handrail on the spiral staircase that leads to the gallery. The client was nervous at first of damaging the floor by walking on it in heels, but in fact it looks even better once it picks up a patina of use – just as a saddle does.*

OPPOSITE BOTTOM LEFT *The artist's impression produced to show the client how the leather-clad library would look, complete with coffered ceiling. The grey flannel curtains shown are those used in winter, as opposed to the sheer silk ones shown in the photograph (opposite top) that are used in summer.*

OPPOSITE BOTTOM RIGHT *The top of the leather chimney breast, leading the eye up to the coffered ceiling. The warm colours and textures create a feeling of intimacy and cosiness, even though the dimensions are so huge.*

ROOM BOARD *This is the board for the library-cum-trophy room in the house on a stud farm featured in the photograph (opposite top). Using this we were able to commission the artist's impression (opposite bottom left), and show the client what we planned to achieve in this magnificent double-height space.*

Leather was always going to dominate this scheme and it has been used by Bill Amberg to stunning effect for the floor, the chimney breast and the curtain poles, finials and hand-stitched rings (6). Other rich textures introduced into the room include the cushions in wool (7) and cashmere (10), and the suede (14) on the sofa. A patterned cushion flap (11) on the wool cushion is cashmere. The wood finish in wenge (9) is at the core of the scheme, used for the joinery and staircase.

Furniture needed to be a mix of comfortable seating provided by the 'Opium' chairs (5) and the 'Bellini' sofa (8), along with the more masculine 'Barbuda' armchair (17), all by Christian Liaigre. There is also an oriental influence here, apparent in the horseshoe chair (16), Chinese coffee table (12) and Chinese vellum trunks (3). A wooden stepladder (13) is both practical and visually interesting.

It was important to introduce some decorative forms, so the room did not appear austere, from the curtain finials and accessories by McKinney & Co (1 and 2) to the traditional side tables (15). Table lamps with a frosted glass base from Donghia (4) are the ideal choice in a room that has the aura and calm of a gentleman's club.

Something old, something new

THE CHALLENGE: To take an Arts & Crafts period house and gently lead it into the twenty-first-century, without falling foul of conservation regulations.

THE SOLUTION: To accept the constraints inherent in the architecture and work with them rather than fighting them, while allowing the mind to think laterally.

KEY CONSIDERATIONS

Turning an Arts & Crafts house into a stylish twenty-first century home.

Being sympathetic to the period architecture.

Researching what elements of the house could and could not be changed.

Finding a way of imposing balance on awkwardly proportioned rooms.

Revitalizing existing pieces of treasured family furniture and giving them a new look.

Thinking laterally to find workable solutions.

This client came to me with an interesting problem. She was now living in her old family home with all its wonderful memories, but she wanted to move it forward in design terms. However, it was a listed house of the Arts & Crafts period, so there were lots of restrictions on what a designer could or could not do. What was needed was a sympathetic approach, a way of giving the house the equivalent of cosmetic surgery without losing any of its wonderful charm and character.

Although we had to be very careful not to destroy any of the house's protected architectural features, we were able to add an extention on at the back, creating a contemporary kitchen and family living space that was what our client needed most, with four young children to bring up. However, upstairs the bedrooms had to be kept as they were when she herself was growing up there. The house was full of family memories for her, so it was important to make sure we did nothing that would destroy the inherent feeling of the place, while also trying to give it the modern look she now wanted.

One of the biggest challenges was that the original fireplace in the living room was both off-centre and adjacent to the door, meaning the room lacked symmetry. It could not be moved or replaced, so instead I looked for ways of imposing balance upon the space. Rather than worry that the seating could not be lined up around the fireplace, I simply moved it down the room and then used three tall vases to make a visual link between the fireplace and the other end of the room. I also researched carefully what could be altered, discovering that we could replace the fire surround and box, as long as we kept the original mantelpiece.

By staining floors and doors dark, adding in low-level lighting and re-covering chairs that had been passed down through the family, it was possible to make the house look significantly different. People often assume I love only contemporary as opposed to period architecture, but in fact I love both – as my own nineteenth-century home shows. One of the things I loved most about this project was finding imaginative solutions to its quirkiness, such as suitable window treatments for tiny triangular windows.

OPPOSITE *The hall has been transformed through staining the floors, doors and stairs black. Two enormous pendant lights made of horn, from Ochre, add a wow factor.*

ABOVE *Although most of the house had to be kept structurally as it was, it was possible to build on a new kitchen and family room to the rear. Although contemporary in style, with a 'Long Courrier' dining table and 'Pastora' lights by Christian Liaigre, this also reflects the original design ethos of the house.*

RIGHT *A plan of the ground floor of the house shows both the original parts of the building and the new-build where the kitchen and family living/dining room are now located.*

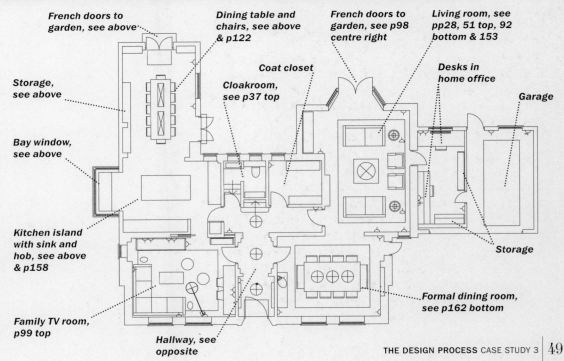

French doors to garden, see above

Dining table and chairs, see above & p122

French doors to garden, see p98 centre right

Living room, see pp28, 51 top, 92 bottom & 153

Storage, see above

Coat closet

Cloakroom, see p37 top

Desks in home office

Garage

Bay window, see above

Kitchen island with sink and hob, see above & p158

Storage

Family TV room, p99 top

Formal dining room, see p162 bottom

Hallway, see opposite

ROOM BOARD This is the board produced for the living room shown opposite top. A neutral canvas was created using a textured plaster finish (1), Perfect Taupe paint (2) and the floor stained to a dark wenge finish (13). A stone finish (8) was chosen for the fireplace, which was brought up to date by installing the contemporary firebox (9).

The rug (19) was chosen for its rich texture, but in a light cream colour (18), and bound in cream leather (6). Furnishing fabrics are mainly velvets, used on the renovated chairs (12) and darker-toned cushions (5 and 10). Cushion bands are made of silk (4) and suede (11); the latter is embellished with horn buttons. Velvet is complemented by a loose-weave linen on the curtains (7), hung on a pole (15) with decorative finials made of wood from McKinney & Co (14).

Additional glamorous touches have been introduced through crystal bowls by Anna Torfs (3), scagliola bowls by McCollin Bryan (16) and the black glass globes with decorative feet from CC Glass (17). In the final scheme (see opposite), a stunning 'Frozen Water' bowl by Amanda Brisbane makes a sculptural statement on the coffee table.

OPPOSITE TOP The fireplace in the living room was listed and so could not be moved, but it was off-centre to the room. Staining it dark and replacing the firebox gave it a more contemporary look. The space next to it was then punctuated with three tall vases, giving the room a feeling of balance that had hitherto been lacking.

OPPOSITE BOTTOM LEFT The staircase is a protected feature of the house, but it was possible to stain the treads dark and add a contemporary runner. This was banded at the edges rather than taking it to the full width of the stairs. Low-level lighting is practical in a house with young children and adds a modern touch.

OPPOSITE BOTTOM CENTRE When it came to working with the Arts & Crafts architecture, it was a matter of thinking laterally to find workable solutions. For example, the bedrooms have many interesting period features that could not be altered, such as these small triangular windows. Pieces of fabric that can be folded up and attached with hooks make attractive and ingenious curtains.

OPPOSITE BOTTOM RIGHT It was important in a family home to come up with ideas for every member of the family. In one of the children's bedrooms, this custom-designed single shelf makes an ideal place for much-loved books next to the bed. The bookend within the design keeps them safely in place.

ABOVE *Internal architecture often sets the style signature for the rest of the house. This wooden staircase brings strong graphic lines to this calming and welcoming holiday home.*

DESIGN AND DECORATION

The first step of the design process is to consider the architectural elements within the room – these are, in effect, the bone structure that holds everything else together. If you have original features, you need to think how best to integrate them into your decorative scheme. If there are no features, or only mediocre ones, you might look for ways of introducing them, perhaps by replacing doors, revamping staircases or installing wall panelling. Architectural elements are also a way of improving the proportions of a space. Get this right and you create a strong base for your other design ideas.

Doors

The first impression of your home and an integral part of the internal architecture, doors deserve careful consideration.

To me, the door has become integral to a scheme – much more than just an architectural necessity.

I don't even think of doors as doors, but as scaled-up panels against the wall. They are a fantastic place on which to play with textural contrast. If you are lucky enough to own a period property with superb original doors, you will probably wish to leave them alone. If, on the other hand, you have a house or flat with very few architectural features, you can create some of your own by either changing or embellishing the doors. Given the choice, I will always replace conventionally sized doors with really tall ones – they add such impact to the look of a room. It doesn't matter whether a room is large, medium or small: fit the biggest doors that you can. If the ceiling is too low, take the doors right to its edge – you will make a room appear taller than it is. You don't have to hang doors in the conventional way, either. You can pivot them from the centre, slide them into place or camouflage them completely against a wall.

Doors don't have to be made of wood – they can equally be glass, metal, covered in fabric or virtually any other material. I might clad them in leather or cover them with a plaster finish, add panels of paper or inlay them with marquetry. When it comes to texture, density and depth, the door is a fitting place to start.

BELOW LEFT *This black stained oak front door is in effect a Mondrian-style artwork created out of wood. It appears monumental, but in fact the door itself is on a conventional scale inset into the imposing surround.*

BELOW *One of the things I try to avoid when designing halls is a room full of nondescript doors. Here I replaced them with sliding screens constructed from wooden frames and leather panels, which create an elegant backdrop for furniture and paintings while hinting at the rooms beyond.*

OPPOSITE *Traditionally crafted shoji create an air of mystery with diffused light illuminating the internal garden. Made by Miya Shoji, from linden wood that has been lacquered black, they are assembled without nails or screws, using traditional joinery methods.*

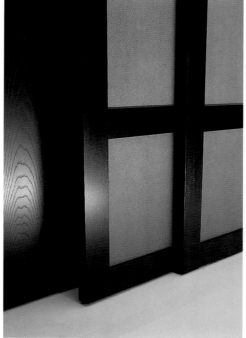

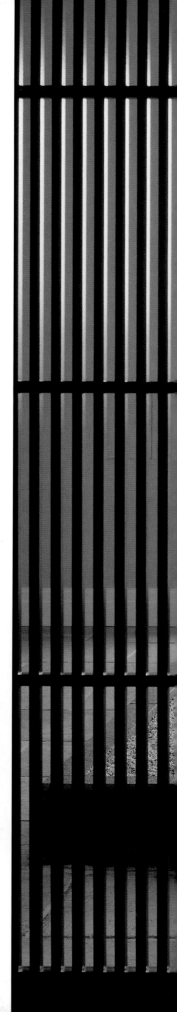

The door is a great place to play. When I begin designing, one of the first things I ask myself is 'What can I do with the doors?' Here are some points to consider:

Scale Big, big, big is the way to go. Absolutely nothing changes the look of a room faster than replacing conventionally sized doors with super-tall double ones.

How to hang If you are replacing doors, you don't have to hang new ones in the conventional way. Doors can slide, pivot, concertina or revolve.

Style Doors don't have to be doors; they can be replaced with panels, such as Japanese-style shoji ones.

Material Doors are usually made of wood, but they can also be constructed from metal, leather, glass or clad with something soft such as linen or paper.

Contrast Choose your material and then think of ways to provide a textural contrast, such as soft gauze slipped between panes of glass or wrought iron with leather.

Door furniture Handles, knobs and such like provide another opportunity to introduce textural contrast and are one of the easiest ways of revamping existing doors.

BELOW Creating door furniture that looks like runners is a classic Kelly Hoppen treatment. In this case, I used oblongs of brushed steel on wooden doors that have been stained black.

BELOW Patinated metal door furniture adds a further layer of character to contemporary dark stained oak doors. Their almost medieval look is an unexpected touch in a new home with a very contemporary style.

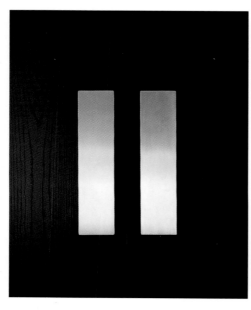

ABOVE Door furniture can be made from as many different materials as the doors themselves. Here the handles of wooden joinery have been re-covered in stitched leather to complement a leather trophy room.

ABOVE Textural contrast between door and door furniture is always effective – here pale painted wooden doors have been complemented by round door knobs of smoky coloured glass.

ABOVE LEFT If the proportions of your home allow, consider replacing existing single doors with extra-tall double ones. Here glass panels and dark wood are reminiscent of those found in French chateaux.

ABOVE Look for ways to make something really individual. In this chic bathroom feathered paper has been sandwiched between the glass on each side, creating doors that have a semi-translucent look.

LEFT Panels in doors make a point of interest, but they don't have to be conventional in shape. The slats in these beautifully architectural doors create an oriental feel in keeping with the library beyond.

KELLY SAYS

Doors are the new chimney breasts – the place where you can introduce something exciting and unexpected.

Fireplaces

Fireplaces are more than architectural features – they make a room feel more welcoming.

If you have an existing working fireplace, then keep it. There is absolutely nothing better on a cold winter's day than walking into a room where there is a real fire burning. Not surprisingly, fireplaces are traditionally a focal point within a room, but that doesn't mean you can't replace a mediocre period one with something more contemporary and striking. If you do opt to keep an original design, introduce contrast by juxtaposing it with something edgy and modern. Even if a fireplace is not in working order, it will still bring another dimension to a space – I have created several faux fireplaces for clients, which have undeniably made a room more characterful and welcoming.

Chimney breasts are a great place to introduce an element of textural contrast, such as a different wall finish or specialist plaster. However, in today's homes they are also the natural location for plasma television screens. Don't be tempted to camouflage these behind fake art or any other novelty treatment. A chic screen housed in the wall looks perfectly acceptable today.

FAR LEFT *By setting a modern firebox into the plaster finish of a centrally placed flue, the comfort and character of an open fire can be enjoyed from both the bedroom and bathroom of this master suite.*

ABOVE LEFT *A comfortable banquette has been positioned directly in front of this contemporary firebox design. Visually it brings the fire further into the room.*

LEFT *In a room where there are no original features, a faux fireplace has been created from a metal surround from which chainmail hangs.*

THIS PAGE *In my own living area, I chose a fire without a conventional mantel, so that it creates a simple panel against the wall. The fire is echoed by the proportions of the plasma screen above.*

Stairs

Part of the intrinsic architecture of the house, staircases can also become flights of fantasy.

THIS PAGE *The stained oak staircase designed for this modern apartment has a sense of form and movement that in essence elevates it to a piece of sculpture. The way it commands the eye makes it the ideal backdrop for displaying art, such as this work by Robert Kombas.*

Staircases are the centre of the home, the pivot around which everything else circles. They are one of the most expensive features to replace, but where clients have agreed, it has been possible to commission some spectacular designs that have absolutely made a scheme.

Staircases do not have to be situated in halls. There is one in my own living room that leads up to a snug. Without it, the room would lose the lion's share of its character and impact. In a room with very high ceilings, you need vertical structures to balance the proportions. I love working with double-height rooms, and stairs are a way of making such spaces come together.

They also provide an opportunity to do something creative. It takes a big budget to commission your own design, but you can make an existing one look custom-built by changing features such as finials, stair rods or banisters. Even something as simple as staining the wood a different colour or adding a stair runner can change the look completely. Lighting can also be used: add low-level spots at tread level to wash the stairs in soft light – this is both atmospheric at night and a safety feature. Stairs are often ignored when it comes to design, too often seen as a functional necessity rather than a three-dimensional form with which to play. So free your imagination and look for a way to create something special out of a piece of internal architecture that is integral to your home.

ABOVE RIGHT *In a house that is custom-designed, it is possible to make the staircase a pivotal point of the internal architecture. The graphic black and white lines of this one create an interesting internal view.*

RIGHT *The simple beauty of a solid glass newel is like the perfect piece of jewellery added to a classic outfit.*

FAR RIGHT *Each component of the staircase should be considered in its own right. Here leather banisters, hand-stitched by Bill Amberg, are the pièce de résistance on a spiral staircase in a leather library.*

Floors

The floor is such a dominant ingredient within the scheme that it is important to choose one that has lasting appeal.

Many people will be surprised to learn that floors are often one of the last subjects I consider in the design process. Before I can decide what to put on the floor, I need to know what is on the walls and of which materials the furniture is comprised. To me, floors are another opportunity to introduce layers of texture into a scheme, so I need to know how they will play visually against all the other key design ingredients. I don't view the floor as one big blank space, but as something on which to create drama. Floors may come late to my schemes, but they are often the making of a room. Poured concrete, leather, terrazzo, slate, rubber, glossed wood, grass matting, shag-pile carpet – there are so many possibilities and they all bring their own character into a scheme.

My signature when designing for clients is to combine hard surfaces or to introduce contrasting textures and colours. I particularly like to design runners and panels within the floor, such as a white stone runner inset into a black stone floor, or a thick square of carpet inlaid in a wooden floor. The result is visually strong and has the effect of leading the eye through the room. Carpet, too, offers its own potential. Smooth carpet has an architectural quality that is almost Art Deco in style, while shag pile – which I have used in my own bedroom – contrasts brilliantly with ultra-modern pieces of furniture. It is also the practical choice in a home where you want to deaden sound. But for me the 'little black dress' of flooring is matting – it always looks chic and it can suit so many styles and rooms, while fitting with every budget.

RIGHT *Being such a big expanse, the floor is an ideal place on which to introduce contrasting materials. Here pebble resin makes a visual and textural play against the surrounding density of polished basalt tiles from Byrock.*

OPPOSITE *Because of the fashion for all things retro, textured and patterned carpets, like this example from Am Collections, are very much in vogue. Not only do they imprint character upon a room, but they are warm and practical, too.*

Don't be influenced by fashion when choosing your floor. You might want to change it in a few years' time, which is not only extremely costly, but means weeks of upheaval and disruption as rooms are stripped of their furniture so that old floors can be taken up and new ones put down.

LEFT *Carpet is enjoying a well-deserved renaissance, especially in bedrooms where it introduces another layer of comfort and sensuality. In my own bedroom I chose a soft shag-pile carpet in pure wool, which imbues the space with a feeling of warmth and luxury. In addition, carpet is an ideal material with which to deaden noise, making it a practical flooring choice in modern urban settings, particularly in apartments.*

ABOVE *Each of these extra-wide reclaimed oak floorboards was hand-chosen for this architect-built house. Stained black, they create the most extraordinary foundation for the scheme. Boards such as this have a very masculine character, but here they have been balanced with the* femininity of the soft furnishings, such as the linen curtains *that fall in pools to the floor, the silk woven cushions on the chairs and the velvet devoré bedspread. The large cream rug serves to ground the bed within the room and adds to the sense of comfort.*

LEFT *In a guest cloakroom, an old stone floor is inset with a runner of black reclaimed floorboards. The effect is mirrored with the specially commissioned lightbox above, designed by Simon Page, which houses a collection of antique snuff bottles from Robert Hall.*

OPPOSITE TOP LEFT *Extra-wide borders on carpet create a striking effect, particularly when chosen for textural contrast, such as this leather one teamed with a luxurious wool-and-silk carpet in a chequerboard effect. A taupe wooden floor is the perfect foil.*

OPPOSITE TOP RIGHT *Leather floors look sensational, but it is also an excellent material to use as a border for carpets and runners. Here faux crocodile makes a bold visual statement against a silk-and-linen carpet layered over a grey stone floor.*

OPPOSITE BOTTOM LEFT *Polished limestone is an ideal companion to reclaimed floorboards that have been stained black – both materials have an individual beauty, but when laid together they create a harmony of yin stone and yang wood, giving them new relevance.*

OPPOSITE BOTTOM RIGHT *This bed is set on a luxurious wool carpet bordered with leather floating on a rich wood floor. The washed linen bedspread is laid so as to provide additional texture and colour against the floor, almost becoming part of the flooring design.*

STONE VERSUS WOOD

These two classic materials still dominate contemporary schemes. They mix with each other beautifully well, but if you do want to choose just one to work with, these pointers may help:

Style Stone is unbeatable in a truly minimalist interior, but make sure it is laid to perfection. Wood, particularly when it is stained black, also looks great, but has the advantage of being more laid-back in character.

Maintenance Stone can stain easily and is hard to renovate. Wood can simply be resanded if it is damaged.

Warmth Stone is a cooler material, but it is perfect to use with underfloor heating because it radiates trapped heat, whereas wood tends to absorb it.

Expense Neither stone nor wood comes cheap, but you may be able to salvage existing wooden floorboards.

Flexibility Once you have made your choice of stone, it is final. Wooden floors, however, can be resanded or repainted relatively easily if you want a whole new look in years to come.

Durability If they are well looked after, both wood and stone can last and last.

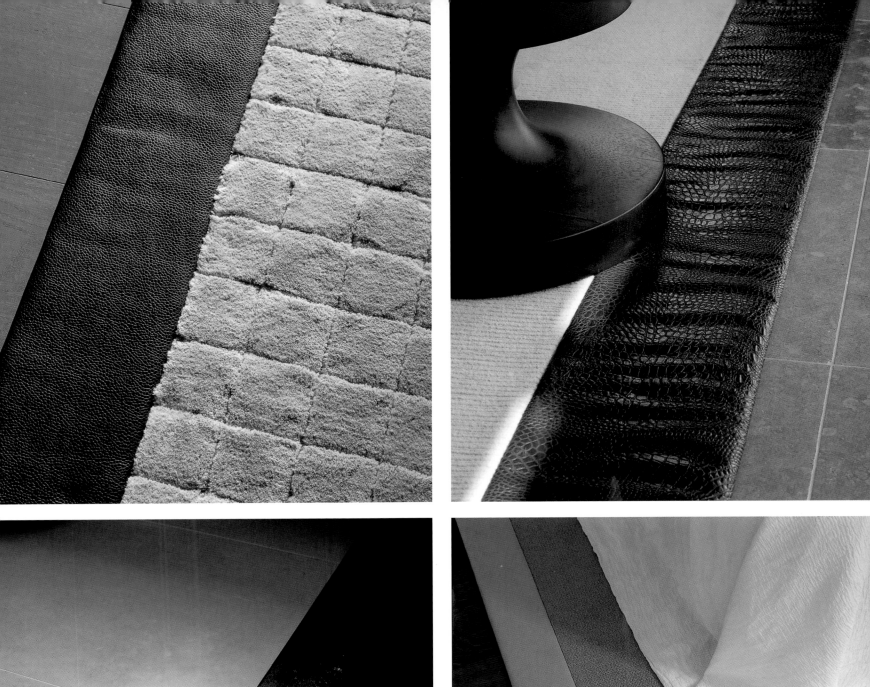

Walls

Walls should be objects of beauty in their own right, but also enhancing scene-setters to pieces of furniture and art.

The first thing you have to decide when choosing wall treatments is whether anything is to be hung on the wall. If you have a collection of art, then the wall needs to be a backdrop to this, not in competition with it. If, on the other hand, the wall itself is to be a focal point, then you can push out the boundaries when deciding how to cover it.

Walls are a great place to add texture, whether through something contemporary such as a specialist plaster finish, or through something more retro in feel such as bold flocked wallpaper. In a modern house with barely any architectural features, for example, you can inject interest with panels of fabric or feature walls of old brick. Walls are all about creating surprises, so engender excitement with overscaled images or unexpected accent colours. In my own schemes I am continually looking for ways of doing something different with walls, whether it is lacquering them a deep oriental red or panelling them with leather, walling them in linen or coating them in gold wax. The only restriction is your own imagination.

RIGHT *In this modern apartment silver leaf has been applied to the walls and then distressed to give it a sense of age. It is a treatment that bestows a touch of glamour, while still allowing the art, by Desiree Dolron on the left and Vanessa Beecroft on the right, to take centre stage.*

SPECIALIST PLASTER

This is the couture equivalent of wall decoration, because it is possible to commission precisely the look that you want, be it straight, crinkled, geometric, knobbly or wavy. You can also have it made in the colour of your choice and blend in more than one shade. There are now many specialist plasterers to choose from, so prices have dropped in recent years – if you want real expertise, the Italians still have the edge over everyone else. I love using plaster because it adds extra depth to a scheme, as well as colour and pattern.

OPPOSITE *The wall of this monochrome dining room has been coated with textured plaster mixed with marble dust, natural spices and natural pigment to achieve the feel of stone. Its beauty is highlighted by the dark wood floor and table and Christian Liaigre's 'Velin' chair.*

ABOVE *Plaster can be used to create pattern and introduce subtle colour to a scheme. Here textured plaster mixed with cement dust and natural pigment has been worked into squares.*

ABOVE RIGHT *This is a detail of the dining room shown opposite, with the walls coated in textured plaster. As a material, it is a great foil to other textures, such as the lustrous metal surface of this lamp and vase.*

RIGHT *This wall has been coated with smooth plaster dyed with a natural pigment and then polished with gold-powder wax. The end result is a slick, precious and silky surface that imbues the room with a feeling of glamour.*

RIGHT *Here the wall has been coated with textured plaster composed of Fiji sand, gold dust and natural pigments. The shiny surface of the enamelled ceramic stool by India Mahdavi brings out the grainy quality of the plaster.*

OPPOSITE *Textured plaster mixed with marble dust and natural pigments has been used to coat this wall. The combed finish has the effect of vibrating light over its surface, adding another dimension of interest. This is reflected in the metal sculpture by Megaron.*

KELLY'S INSIDER SECRETS

If you are lucky enough to have high ceilings, draw the eye up even further with great vertical sweeps of colour or texture.

To make a room appear bigger, accentuate its width through horizontal bands.

Pale colours make walls recede, while dark ones bring them in.

If you want to camouflage doors, look for a wall treatment that can do just that – such as wood panelling or fabric walling.

Remember that whatever colour or texture is chosen for the walls, the ceiling must blend with it.

KELLY SAYS

If you use paint on walls, use the same colour on the woodwork and ceiling – it's like wearing black tights and black shoes with a black dress.

Storage

At the heart of successful design is an acknowledgement that everything should have its rightful place.

If you want a home that is not only well designed but also easy to maintain, then you must consider storage as part of the design process. You need to differentiate between storage and display, though many pieces of furniture combine the two. Storage is about creating space in which to keep essential goods and objects that are often not in themselves intrinsically beautiful. Display (see pages 133–5) is about drawing the eye to those objects you have chosen for their visual impact.

Ask yourself also whether you want built-in storage or the freestanding variety. The first needs to be planned and installed much earlier in the design process. In effect, it becomes part of the internal architecture of a room. The second really comes under the heading of furniture and is brought into a room at a much later stage, usually when the floors have been put down. Built-in storage can be designed specifically for your needs and the particular items you wish to store, but don't imagine it is a cheaper alternative. Cabinetry is one of the most expensive elements of design – you cannot cut corners, or

ABOVE LEFT *This couture marquetry coffee table was made by Linley. It includes lined drawers where games are kept and is used to display candlesticks by Anna Torfs and bowls by McCollin Bryan.*

ABOVE *In a dining area storage should be both functional and aesthetically pleasing, achieved here by the combination of open shelves and closed cabinets.*

OPPOSITE *This walnut monolith of custom-built storage leaves nothing on display, so it doubles as a wall dividing the hall from the dining room.*

RIGHT As with any other pieces of furniture, storage should be chosen to complement the style of the room. Here Japanese-style shoji panels are a less rigid solution to conventional cupboard doors in an elegant Eastern-inspired dressing room.

BELOW Floor-to-ceiling cupboards are the most efficient way of utilizing space. Here classic Chinese screens of stained oak are an elegant alternative to ordinary cupboard doors in a chic dressing room.

BELOW RIGHT In my own walk-in dressing room, open shelves are a convenient and inexpensive storage solution for clothes and shoes. The success of an arrangement such as this depends on having the discipline to maintain possessions well and keep them tidy.

ABOVE *When it comes to cupboards and drawers, my advice is to choose handles carefully. They are a great way to transform utilitarian furniture into something beautiful, as with these leather-and-wood ones, custom-made for this bathroom furniture.*

ABOVE *Cigarette-shaped horn handles from Ochre add a note of glamour to a stained wood cabinet in a bathroom. It is not just texture that it is important to consider when choosing handles, but form as well – these emphasize the horizontal planes of the scheme.*

KELLY SAYS

Storage doesn't have to mean deep cupboards or large cabinets – a simple shelf, if well located, can make all the difference.

you will end up with something shoddy. It is why a truly minimalist scheme is so expensive to do compared with something more bohemian and laid-back. Freestanding furniture can be made to commission, but good designs are available on the high street. You can paint it, stain it or replace items such as handles to create a more individual look.

You also need to think about whether you want storage that is part of the scheme or, in effect, invisible. Many of my clients ask me to provide cupboard space, but to camouflage it into the walls. This is possible to do, but, again, it comes at a high price because hidden doors are dependent on superb standards of workmanship.

The only way to design storage that really works is to write a list itemizing which activities each room is used for and which related objects need to be stored there, whether it is DVDs in the living room or cotton buds in the bathroom. Where possible, choose solutions that offer a degree of flexibility, such as shelves that can be moved up or down, or drawer dividers that make it possible to use every inch of space effectively.

If you can, install integral lighting – not only so you can see where everything is, but because it is effectively another source of atmospheric lighting, particularly in furniture that combines display. If you wish to light a piece of freestanding storage furniture, such as a bookcase, one simple trick is to fit an architectural tube on top, which will gently illuminate the area. Washing light down from the ceiling onto the front of shelves also brings objects such as books to life.

Because cabinetry is so costly, it can work out cheaper to design walk-in storage. In my own apartment I was lucky enough to have space for a walk-in dressing room. Since it was a purpose-built space, I saved thousands of pounds by deciding against cupboard doors – instead, my clothes are hung on open rails or folded on open shelves. I mention this because what appears to be a touch of luxury actually cost very little when compared with the standard row of built-in wardrobes.

Storage may be part of the nuts and bolts of a room, but when planned well it adds another point of interest within a room.

EIGHT STEPS TO A MORE ORGANIZED LIFE

1 Buy nothing new unless you know exactly where it is going to go within your home.

2 Make sure everything you own has its place.

3 Store items that you rarely use out of sight.

4 Edit your possessions regularly: recycle unwanted goods to charities that can benefit.

5 Never put anything away that is damaged or dirty.

6 Have containers of the same scale for the items stored – from large such as bedding to small such as paper clips.

7 Label all storage boxes, so you can find what you want easily.

8 Accept that if you haven't used or worn something for two years, the chances are you never will.

Layers of warmth

THE CHALLENGE: To create the perfect getaway for family and friends in a chalet high in the mountains that would be both practical and luxurious.

THE SOLUTION: To build the main rooms around real fires, pale wood and layers of heavenly textures.

KEY CONSIDERATIONS

Achieving a design that would be practical, easy to maintain and comfortable in the extreme.

Being inspired by winter, snow and mountain views.

Making the most of wonderful clear natural light.

Building the major rooms around fires that could be enjoyed from all angles.

Using wood as the dominant material to create a feeling of warmth and cosiness.

Enhancing that feeling by using layers of luxurious and tactile textures.

Engendering a sense of total relaxation.

ABOVE LEFT *The chimney flue between the living room and kitchen, with table and 'Velin' banquettes and chairs by Christian Liaigre, has been used to house the plasma screen. The fire itself is the pivotal point of the room.*

The flue and firebox were specially commissioned for the house, the circular log store to the side. Cosy textures, such as leather, suede and mohair, have been chosen for seating and cushions.

ROOM BOARD *This mountain location demanded warm, luxurious bedrooms. The taupe wood finish (27) on the beams and floorboards (26) combines with a darker finish (13) used for furniture. On the walls is a specialist plaster (20), accented by pure white paint (4). Sheer linen curtains (18) and the textured silk rug (22) form a foundation for other fabrics, including* the creamy linen (23) used on the headboard (2), the cashmere bed throw (17) and cushions in pony (10), herringbone linen (14) and aged leather (15) banded in linen (5). Mother-of-pearl buttons (14) add further layering. Taupe leather has been used for the frame of the dressing-table mirror (7) and a paler shade for the stool (16), complemented by horn vases (9). *Other accessories include ceramics (11) and globe vases that I designed for Wedgwood (8 and 24), with white plate coral (12 and 25). Reading lights from Chad (3) contrast with the feathered wall light from Ochre (1). The punched pony bed base (6) is a key feature of the bedroom; in the bathroom it is the stone 'Baja' bath from Antonio Lupi (19) in finish (21).*

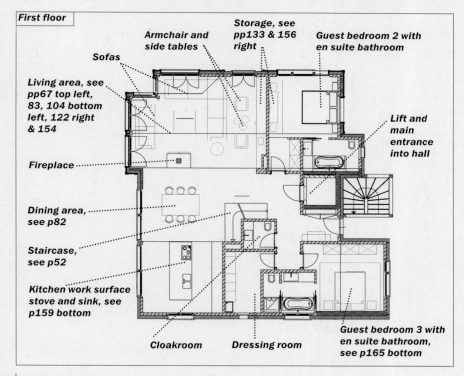

First floor

- Armchair and side tables
- Storage, see pp133 & 156 right
- Guest bedroom 2 with en suite bathroom
- Sofas
- Living area, see pp67 top left, 83, 104 bottom left, 122 right & 154
- Lift and main entrance into hall
- Fireplace
- Dining area, see p82
- Staircase, see p52
- Kitchen work surface stove and sink, see p159 bottom
- Cloakroom
- Dressing room
- Guest bedroom 3 with en suite bathroom, see p165 bottom

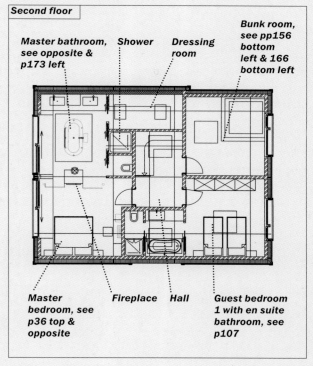

Second floor

- Master bathroom, see opposite & p173 left
- Shower
- Dressing room
- Bunk room, see pp156 bottom left & 166 bottom left
- Master bedroom, see p36 top & opposite
- Fireplace
- Hall
- Guest bedroom 1 with en suite bathroom, see p107

I was delighted when these clients asked me to create a very special interior for their chalet, because it was something that was clearly so dear to their hearts – a holiday home that they would share with family and friends. A home that is also a holiday destination requires a different approach altogether, because it needs to be simple enough that when you arrive you can just unpack and start to enjoy yourself – so on one level it needs to be very practical. However, it is also somewhere that has to make you feel cosseted and spoilt, so you have a feeling of really getting away from it all and leaving your cares behind you.

The key to achieving both lies in the materials chosen. I used taupe wood throughout – for the ceilings, floors and shutters – because there really is nothing cosier than wood, so it created a cocoon into which I could introduce wintry textures such as velvet, mohair, cashmere and suede. The views are stunning, so I kept window treatments simple, allowing bright mountain light to flood into the rooms. Real fires are also a must, and I placed these centrally so that downstairs one could be enjoyed from both the living area and the kitchen, and in the master suite from both the bedroom and bathing areas. Flues for these proved the perfect place to mount plasma screens both upstairs and downstairs.

ABOVE The bedroom and bathroom of the master suite are divided only by the chimney flue, making it possible to enjoy the fire from both. The headboard is upholstered in a punctured cowhide known as pony.

RIGHT The bathing side of the master suite: milk-glass doors at the far end lead to a loo on one side and shower on another. Wooden shutters and flowing linen curtains allow light to flood into the entire room.

ABOVE *A small bronze side table with delicate legs sits happily next to an antique chair covered in suede, with a Fortuny silk cushion. The carpet is also made of silk.*

FURNI TURE AND FURN ISHINGS

It is now time to get down to the nitty-gritty of the decorative scheme. This is your chance to play around with lots of samples of fabrics, flooring, paint and so forth and work out what you want to use where. Gather all the design references you can, from furniture shapes to curtain headings. Spend the time and energy on this that your home deserves and you will create something very special indeed.

Furniture

Much more than a functional necessity, furniture brings together the key ingredients of colour, texture and form.

THIS PAGE Be bold about mixing different shapes and textures when it comes to furniture. Here an animal-print leather carver makes an interesting companion to simple white leather dining chairs in a cowhide effect. Both chairs and the table are my own design, while the mirror propped against the wall is by India Mahdavi.

OPPOSITE This bright yellow chair, wrapped in velvet right down to the legs, is a star piece in my own living room, placed against a retro-looking wooden screen of my own design.

FORM

Furniture is currently enjoying a new appreciation. In design terms, it is right at the heart of exciting, vibrant and stimulating interiors. For too long it was something of a poor relation to fabrics and walls, but now people are waking up to the fact that a star piece of furniture can have just as big an impact on a room as sensational artwork.

To me, it is all about form and how one thing relates to something else in the room. I have always enjoyed playing fabrics off against each other – dense velvet with translucent organza, luxurious silk with coarse scrim – but now I like to play with shape and scale. What interests me is to set a curve against a straight line, an extravagantly sculptural shape next to a monastically simple one, an overscaled piece adjacent to a diminutive one. It is an exciting process to see how you can bring out a different quality in a piece of furniture according to what it is juxtaposed with – it is why I love to mix vintage and antique finds with designs at the cutting edge of contemporary furniture.

This love of form means I work in a slightly unusual way when designing. Whereas other people will look at a plan of the room and try to work out how best to fit in a prescriptive list of furniture – sofa, coffee table, bookcase and so on – I start with the star piece of furniture I am longing to use and try every trick I can to make it work in the given space. The first way might be more rational, but, to me, design should be all about using the things you love and that you are excited by.

Furniture is also about texture, an opportunity to create interest with contrasting materials, such as faux crocodile with metal or a zingy velvet with lacquer. Clients often ask

OPPOSITE TOP LEFT *Individual pieces are a way of introducing visual play into a room, as with this antique Chinese chair. Its ornate shape is set against the grid of the French windows.*

OPPOSITE TOP RIGHT *The organic shape of the ceramic stool and leather chairs by India Mahdavi makes them an interesting addition to a contemporary family room. The colours and textures play against the plaster finish on the walls and artwork by Desiree Dolron.*

OPPOSITE BOTTOM LEFT *For one of my own chair designs, I chose linen upholstery and used chainmail as a contemporary interpretation of traditional fringing and as a way of layering up texture. The wooden stool is by Bleu Nature.*

OPPOSITE BOTTOM RIGHT *The form and proportion of furniture can also be used to reflect that of the room in which it sits, as with the antique lacquered Chinese bench placed in a corner of this elegant dining room.*

ABOVE LEFT *It is possible to make more of a piece of furniture through the way it is upholstered. Here pony – a term used for punched cowhide – gives an embossed look to a simple tub armchair from Modénature.*

LEFT *Just as contrasting textures can be used to create unexpected effects, so can the idea of solidity and translucency. Here a glass 'Ghost' chair by Fiam seems to float on a sea of shag-pile carpet.*

Look for furniture with star quality – the ability to fill a space with pizzazz through form and texture.

me to assimilate existing pieces, such as family heirlooms, into a scheme. It rarely presents a problem – armchairs, for example, take on a new life when re-covered; antique chests look wonderful placed next to really modern sofas.

One of my rules is that there should always be at least two star pieces in a room – the ones that catch the eye and make your heart jolt every time you walk in. They shouldn't necessarily both be furniture, but a piece that provides that wow factor is good value for money. At one end of the scale, it could be something you have commissioned and had made specially; at the other, it could be a salvaged find from a car boot sale or flea market.

THINK OUT OF THE BOX

People are often unimaginative in the way they lay out furniture, grouping all the seating around the fireplace or television, for example. It is much more interesting to have more than one seating area if possible – a formal one for entertaining and a less formal one for reading. Bend the rules – mix furniture of different styles, vintages and textures, and don't position it in the most obvious way. Symmetrical arrangements work best in perfectly proportioned rooms; if this is not the case, remember that balance and harmony are more important than rigid symmetry.

TOP LEFT *The organic form of India Mahdavi's wooden stools plays against the lacquer and chrome Art Deco-style bar that I designed. Faux-crocodile seats add further textural interest. The art on the wall behind is by Desiree Dolron.*

TOP *A beautiful Andrée Putman (for Ralph Pucci) sofa upholstered in pale cream linen is the focal point of a perfectly proportioned* hall. *Note the scale of the cushions, chosen so as not to detract from the sofa's shape and elegance.*

ABOVE *Two oriental-style chairs are placed directly opposite each other, emphasizing the symmetrical proportions of this elegant bedroom. But it is the overscaled floor lamp that is the dynamic ingredient within the scheme, taking the eye both up and out.*

FUNCTION
When it comes to choosing furniture that is essential for living – items such as the sofa, bed or dining chairs – then the only sensible way to do it is by getting out there and trying it for yourself. You simply cannot buy such important investments by flicking through a catalogue or ordering over the Internet. Comfort is all, and you need to know that a sofa is not too deep for you, a bed too soft or a chair too high.

Which style of furniture you choose will naturally come down to the look of the room you have designed. Furniture can be either masculine or feminine: straight-edged and rather austere or curved and embellished. This is a personal choice, though I strive for balance in a room, so like to mix in elements of both.

ABOVE *For the living area in my own apartment, I had two new chairs re-covered in velvet that was not recommended for upholstery use. This has given them a slightly distressed vintage look.*

ABOVE RIGHT *In this television room, imbued with strict two-by-two symmetry, armchairs on pivots have been chosen so that it is possible to position them with* ease *for comfortable viewing. The side tables are by Tucker Robbins.*

RIGHT *This pair of classic wing armchairs, which have been handed down through the family, have been revitalized through the use of different upholstery fabric – a rich silk velvet with a horizontal self-stripe. Banded cushions emphasize the chairs' new modern look.*

ABOVE *In the family dining area of a kitchen, two different types of seating have been used to break up the space. Circular seating echoes the shape of the table from Modénature, which in turn is mirrored by the Kevin Reilly light above. On the wall behind is the stunning gelatine silver collection print by Jean Baptiste Huynh.*

OPPOSITE TOP *This David Gill dining table with its scagliola top is the star piece of a glamorous dining room, with chairs from B&B Italia. Light from the crystal chandelier by Mark Brazier-Jones and from the lacquered bookcase is reflected in the table's surface.*

OPPOSITE BOTTOM *Furniture layouts do not have to be obvious: here two L-shaped sofas are placed opposite each other, accentuating the symmetry of the room. The planks of the coffee table echo the grid-like design.*

You will also be led by space constraints. It amazes me how many people order furniture without checking that the dimensions will fit, not only within the chosen room but also through the front door or up the stairs. You really must do your homework. If you are not skilled with working to scaled plans, then get a roll of masking tape and a tape measure and set to work outlining on the floor the size and shape of the furniture you are planning to buy. Also mark the height on the walls, so you can try to visualize the effect in 3-D. If you do this with every piece of furniture you are hoping to fit in, you will soon get a feeling for whether it is going to work or not – you don't want to end up with a disparate set of jumbled pieces. Bear in mind that you also need to allow sufficient space to move around with ease.

If you are replacing furniture or adding to an existing scheme, it is also worth remembering that any new piece can jar when it is first delivered. A sofa that looked modest in the context of a showroom can look enormous when placed in your own living

space. As long as you have taken the measurements correctly, you probably just need a few days to adjust to its presence. It is quite normal for people to absolutely hate new acquisitions when they first appear, so don't panic – the chances are that after a week or so the room will have 'settled' again.

Budget is also a big part of the furniture-buying process. If you decide to buy a piece of clothing, such as a grey shirt, you first have an idea of what you are looking for and then you go searching for one you can afford. The same applies to furniture. If you want to splash out on a couple of special items, then you might have to economize elsewhere. I would never buy a bed or sofa that is very cheap, because comfort is too important, but items such as tables or cabinets are now available at really competitive prices.

Finally, although it is possible to design around existing pieces of furniture, sometimes it is better to let them go and start again. It can hamper your creativity if you are struggling to make something work that no longer fits with your own sense of the aesthetic.

THIS PAGE *Swathes of parachute silk are complemented by painted Versailles-inspired panelling. A Silent Gliss blind provides privacy and protects furniture from the glare of natural light.*

Windows

Curtains and blinds need to be considered not only for their impact on a room, but as a link to what lies outside.

I have reached a point in my design journey where I prefer less on a window. I used to love to dress them up extravagantly, but now I prefer to put the focus elsewhere – in particular on doors and furniture. I am much more likely to use simple wooden shutters or panels of plain linen or scrim than to hang great swathes of lined and interlined fabric.

Another reason for this is that I have become a light junkie, so I look for window treatments that will encourage light into a room rather than block it out. I like to be woken by light in the morning; it feels more natural and healthy. I realize it doesn't suit everyone, though, so when thinking about window treatments this should be your first consideration: to allow light in or to shut it out.

I would also encourage everyone to embrace the idea of seasonal changes. In summer there is nothing better than shutters flung open to enjoy the light; in winter you might want to hang heavier curtains over these and engender a cosy feeling of hibernation.

ABOVE *A simple Indian voile blends with the soft femininity of this all-white bedroom-cum-living room. The curtain treatments have been kept as unfussy as possible in order not to detract from the calm of the space.*

ABOVE *Glamorous cascades of silk falling in folds to the floor have been given an almost Gothic twist by slashing them – they add a theatrical note to the staircase in my own apartment.*

Finials on poles are like earrings – they add the finishing touch.

LEFT *Yellow borders on the top and bottom of elegant linen curtains accentuate the sunny atmosphere of this garden room. The Chinese trunk echoes the accent colour.*

CENTRE FAR LEFT *Consider how curtains are hung as well as the curtains themselves; here a hand-stitched leather curtain pole is teamed with a sheer grey linen shot through with metallic thread.*

CENTRE LEFT *Rather than hang curtains that end at floor level, create a more fluid effect by taking the drop deeper. These couture-made curtains in loose-weave linen fold elegantly onto the black stained floor.*

BOTTOM FAR LEFT *When dressing a window, curtains can be hung for show only – rather than to be drawn. Here voluminous linen falls to the floor like a fabulous ballgown.*

BOTTOM LEFT *In this peaceful bedroom, lined and interlined sheer curtains are hung over a Roman blind made of linen. The glass pole and finials complement the simplicity of the window treatment.*

BELOW *Windows of unusual shapes or proportions are often best dressed with a blind as opposed to curtains. This classic linen Roman blind imposes linearity on an arched window.*

BLINDS VERSUS CURTAINS

If you are trying to choose between the two, here are a few points to consider:

Style Blinds have a more architectural quality, so they work well in contemporary rooms. Curtains are more fluid in style.

Versatility Blinds are often a better option for awkwardly shaped windows where curtains would be hard to hang.

Materials Blinds are not restricted to fabrics but can be made of other materials such as paper, metal or rattan.

Budget Blinds use less material but are generally more complicated to make, which can push up the price.

Privacy Some types of blind can be used during the day if it is important to screen off the outside world.

Beauty It is hard to beat the aesthetic quality of a curtain made from a glamorous silk or fine linen.

TOP *A pair of Roman linen blinds tied with taupe linen runners accentuate the vertical plane of this symmetrical family room. The scaled-up lamp by Modénature balances this with a strong horizontal line.*

ABOVE *Blinds tied with long runners of fabric is a classic Kelly Hoppen window treatment. At these kitchen windows Petersham ribbon has been used as an accent border on Roman blinds made of linen.*

LEFT *Original shoji blinds made of wood and paper allow light to filter through into a cloakroom, while also ensuring privacy. The grid structure complements the strong shape of the carved stone basin.*

Don't let your imagination be constricted by the notion of trying to achieve simplicity at windows. You can still create something unexpected, if you wish. In my own apartment I have hung panels of chainmail at the windows – light filters through, but the shadows they make on the walls and floor are quite extraordinary. If you do still want to make a big statement with lush curtains, that is fine – but just make sure you keep other decorative elements of the room relatively simple. You need to decide where you want the eye to focus. When I do use curtains, I like to keep them loose as opposed to rigid – ripped silk, perhaps, that falls in decadent pools to the floor.

OPPOSITE *In this incredibly sculptural house built by Munkenbeck & Marshall, I have extended the building's relationship with the garden by fixing plantation shutters to the outside of the windows.*

BELOW *A semi-translucent screen has been attached to this bathroom window, allowing light to filter in while retaining privacy. Tongue-and-groove dado panelling accentuates the architectural feel. The stool is from Modénature.*

ABOVE *For absolute purity and simplicity, it is hard to beat a white painted plantation shutter, such as the one in my own bathroom from New England Shutters. It almost disappears seemlessly into the surrounding walls.*

ABOVE *Cylindrical glass pendant lights from Solzi Luce hang in front of wall-to-wall dark stained wooden shutters in this monochrome bedroom, reflecting light back onto the semi-open slats.*

THIS PAGE *When putting together a soft-furnishing scheme, the important things to consider are tones that harmonize and textures that contrast. The crewelwork cushions here are embellished with horn buttons, so the slightly raised surface of one brings out the smoothness of the other.*

Soft furnishings

Fabrics are at the core of every decorating scheme, but what you do with each is as important as the selection itself.

TOP A linen ottoman with a suede base by Christian Liaigre is a classic combination of tactile fabrics. The zebra rug adds a note of unexpected wildness.

ABOVE Velvet-and-linen striped upholstery fabric is warm to the touch and has a graphic quality that suits the dark stained furniture of this Christian Liaigre 'Opium' chair.

Fabrics are where I begin creating a decorating scheme – though, of course, in practical terms they are the final addition to a room. When I first begin to lay fabrics on a room board, I have few preconceptions. It is only when I have designed the entire scheme that I start to label each one, deciding which is for sofas, curtains, cushions, bedheads and so on. It is a question of setting tones and textures against each other and having a feel for how much or how little of something is needed in a room. Never let one fabric dominate. The trick is to create a family of fabrics where the sum effect is so much greater than its individual parts. I always start with a linen – the core of the fabric family. Without linen, a scheme will never feel quite right. If you long to use a design that is fabulously bright and bold, then limit it to one focal piece of furniture, such as a vintage chair or stool.

Texture is the driving force of everything I do. Without sufficient texture, a neutral scheme will look flat and dead. When working with fabrics, you need many different textures, but from one tonal palette. Collect lots of samples, then try them one against the other until you really understand the effectiveness of contrasting texture. If you think something doesn't look right, get rid of it, even if you love it. Trust your instincts.

When choosing fabrics, you need to think about how a fabric moves. Upholstery fabrics are stationary, so you can opt for something weighty, such as a coarse linen or sinewy velvet. At a window you may prefer something light that moves in the breeze or which lets light filter through – unlined parachute silk, perhaps, or a semi-translucent shoji blind.

Be practical. If you have young children or pets, you need fabrics that can be easily washed. You have to think about maintenance, not just the finished look. Happily, many of the luxurious fabrics that have become so fashionable in recent years, such as suede, leather and animal skin, are now available in very convincing faux versions.

UPHOLSTERY
As a result of my passion for fabrics, I am always on the search for a new way of using them. My love affair with furniture has led me to consider upholstery in a new light, as it is a brilliant way of combining different colours or textures, particularly on an item such as a dining chair where you can choose to have a seat upholstered in a different fabric to the back, or have carvers upholstered in a contrasting material to the rest of the set.

Upholstery is also a way of integrating existing pieces of furniture into a new decorative scheme. Clients often ask me to include antique or inherited pieces, such as traditional wing armchairs. These take on an entirely new look depending on the fabric chosen. One of my favourite techniques is to have chairs 'wrapped' in fabric, which creates something both witty and radical.

Star pieces of furniture, such as vintage chairs, cry out for something special. I sometimes find I have a piece of fabric left on my board that I have not allocated a home to – using it for a focal piece is often the answer. In a neutral scheme it can be fun to shake up the palette with one bright colour or bold pattern.

Budget constraints may mean that you cannot afford to use a fabric you really love on curtains or a big piece of furniture. Instead, it may be possible to use it on a small area, such as a chair back, which will still have impact within the scheme. Adding a touch of luxury in this way can make all the difference to the total effect.

CUSHIONS

One thing of which I never tire is finding great combinations of fabrics and embellishments to use on cushions. Cushions are so inexpensive, freely available in myriad colours and textures on the high street. Yet they can transform the look of a room in seconds, taking it instantly from winter to summer or formal to informal.

One of my signature looks is banding. Take the example of a coarse-linen cushion banded in deep velvet. Not only is this another opportunity to bring in textural contrast, but it is also a simple way of completely changing the look. Take the banding off and you have plain linen, which is summery and relaxed; add the banding and you have a more wintry, cosy feel; swap the banding for a more masculine texture, such as leather, and you instantly create a more edgy ambience. What could be easier?

Embellishment, such as buttons or stitching, is another opportunity to bring in greater textural contrast. You don't need to overdo this. Rather than dress up every single cushion, remember that less is always more. If you have a mix of large and small cushions, it is the small ones that should have most ornamentation, for the simple reason that they are going to be in front of the bigger ones.

I love to use cushions on beds – for me, they finish off the look perfectly. Use six: two big square ones at the back; two standard rectangular ones in the middle; and two tiny ones at the front. You can follow a similar formula when arranging cushions on sofas.

Throws, too, are a wonderfully quick way of changing the feel of a room. I love to snuggle up to sheepskin or soft cashmere in winter, but would always store them away for the summer months. They are really a seasonal addition to the home, but they can be used to introduce a splash of accent colour or to add further textural contrast.

BELOW *The tactile quality of the tufted silk cushion emphasizes the softness of the fine linen curtains and upholstery in this white-on-white summer room.*

BOTTOM *A simple cream linen cushion with a neat buckled band is set on the rich matt of a luxurious dark sheepskin throw, which in turn makes textural play against pale linen upholstery.*

BELOW RIGHT *Bands of fabric in a contrasting colour and texture can change the look of cushions completely, as with these olive velvet bands on plain linen cushions.*

BOTTOM RIGHT *Bolster cushions, such as this faux-crocodile one banded with velvet, are a way of introducing contrast both of form and texture.*

OPPOSITE TOP *Crushed, plain and patterned velvets have been used for the sea of cushions in this family room, with chair and stool by India Mahdavi. The Pop Art-inspired design suits the extrovert scheme, with artworks by Desiree Dolron (left) and Adolf Luther (right).*

OPPOSITE BOTTOM LEFT *A pair of chocolate-brown velvet cushions are placed in front of a leather bolster, each accentuating the tactile qualities of the other.*

OPPOSITE BOTTOM CENTRE *Cushions are a wonderful way of enjoying bursts of colour, such as these jewel-like shades of velvet set against zebra skin.*

OPPOSITE BOTTOM RIGHT *Here orange velvet, accented by a large horn button, provides a burst of colour in an otherwise neutral scheme.*

BEDS

The bed is the focal point of the bedroom, so it makes sense to make a big statement with the bedhead. 'Big' is the key word here. I like ones that are tall and imposing, because they draw the eye upwards, balancing the horizontal proportions of the bed.

In terms of material, you need to choose something that is both eye-catching and comfortable. If, like me, you enjoy sitting in bed to read or watch television, then you need a bedhead that is comfortable to lean back on. That is why my own designs are invariably padded and upholstered. While it is tempting to use a glamorous covering, such as ostrich skin, you do need to think about how you are going to maintain it. I often advise people to use wipeable faux versions of the fabrics they love, particularly in the case of suedes and leathers. You can have loose covers made for bedheads, but I prefer ones that are tightly fitted and tailored.

How much or how little embellishment you add is, of course, a question of personal taste. If you want a really dramatic effect, then remember it is all a question of balance. Choose bedspreads and cushions in more subdued tones, so that everything is not fighting for attention.

All fabrics have their own personality, so whatever you choose for the bedhead will imprint a certain signature on the rest of the room. Do you want a more masculine mood, in which case you may opt for something like chocolate-brown leather or caramel suede? Or do you prefer a feminine look, in which case you may consider white linen or cream cashmere? All other design decisions radiate out from this point, so it's essential to pick the right style for you.

OPPOSITE TOP LEFT *Bedheads are an opportunity to strike a really luxurious and glamorous note within the bedroom. This upholstered design is covered in eelskin, which is complemented by couture plaster walls and fine cotton bedding.*

OPPOSITE BOTTOM LEFT *This bed is set against dark stained wooden shutters that cover a wall of windows. The bedhead is low, so as not to detract from the effect. Six linen cushions with horn buttons are arranged in classic Kelly Hoppen symmetry.*

OPPOSITE TOP RIGHT *In a children's room an exuberant Pop Art-style wallpaper has been used to create a feature wall. Its colours are picked up in the linen bedding, banded cushions and the luxurious sheepskin throw.*

OPPOSITE BOTTOM RIGHT *A very tall panelled headboard upholstered in leather makes a bold statement, complemented by leather and linen cushions and Christian Liaigre's leather 'Grume' bench. The quilted linen bedcover is lined in silk.*

BELOW *In a mountain chalet a combination of knitted fabrics have been used to dress this guest bedroom. The bed design allows it to be used as either a double or two singles.*

KELLY SAYS

I love to use cushions on beds – for me, they finish off the look perfectly. If in doubt, use six: two big square ones at the back, two standard rectangular ones in the middle and two tiny ones at the front.

A dream come true PART 2

THE CHALLENGE: To take a brand-new home and make it feel as though the client had lived there for many years. To create a feeling of warmth and cosiness in a very large house.
THE SOLUTION: To use wonderful combinations of fabrics on furniture, window treatments and accessories to imbue the home with softness and build up layers of comfort.

OPPOSITE TOP The monochrome scheme of this summery living room is very yin and yang with its black stained floor and cream upholstery. The silk carpet and elegant linen curtains add a note of quiet luxury.

OPPOSITE BOTTOM A detail of the room shown above. Boiled-wool cushions make a textural play against linen upholstery. Their tactile quality sets the tone for this welcoming and comfortable room.

ROOM BOARD Fabrics set the mood of the room and here shades of off-white and cream work in quiet harmony, from the darker biscuit tones of the wool cushions (1 and 8) and complementing velvet ones (7) to the milkier tone of the linens (2 and 6) used on other soft furnishings. Mother-of-pearl buttons (1 and 7) set off these fabrics beautifully. These neutrals act as a foil to the dark wood furniture, such as Christian Liaigre's 'Ré' armchairs (13), side tables by Tucker Robbins (14) and the floor lamp (12) – Christian Liaigre's 'Merlot' lamp is used in the final scheme, opposite. Soft linen curtains make a similar contrast against the dark stained curtain pole and decorative finials from McKinney and Co (11). The simplicity of the scheme is echoed in the furniture shapes chosen, from the generous-sized armchairs (3) and sofas (5) upholstered in heavy linen (4), to the oriental influence apparent in the 'Ove' table designed by Eric Schmitt for Christian Liaigre (10) – the table used in the final scheme is by Modénature – and the Chinese cube side tables (9).

KEY CONSIDERATIONS

Making a new home feel established.

Using fabrics to add character and comfort to the interior.

Creating interest through the use of contrasting textures.

Reflecting the use of certain rooms through fabric choices, such as for summer and winter living.

Changing window treatments according to the seasons.

Building up layers of fabrics for a feeling of supreme comfort.

Ensuring a sense of flow from room to room throughout the house.

Not allowing individual designs to overdominate.

If money is tight, visit the fruit and vegetable market and make wonderful arrangements from polished red apples, aubergines or artichokes.

Candles, scented or unscented, are an integral feature of today's homes. What could be better than a relaxing bath by candlelight, or candles lit all round the dining room for a special meal? Candles are not strong enough to be considered light sources in their own right, but as an extra dimension to the general atmosphere they are unbeatable.

Flowers are usually the last ingredient I add to a home, but they are never an afterthought. If I have one piece of advice for a new homemaker, it is to buy vases you love in many sizes, shapes and materials – inexpensive glass and ceramic designs are widely available. You want to feel you can always display flowers well, whatever their variety, colour or number.

I work with the wonderful John Carter, who has put together the most incredible displays of flowers for me for many years. They don't happen by chance. Together we look at fabric swatches and furniture layouts to decide which flowers will have optimum effect in certain settings. Sometimes we choose them for their architectural shape or for their masculine or feminine qualities – at other times it comes down to colour and scent. Some people consider flowers to be an expensive luxury, but to me they are integral to a scheme. It is essential to have something real and organic in your home – without this, it will lack soul. You don't have to splash out on extravagant blooms – something as simple as pots of bulbs or branches of pussy willow makes all the difference.

INSIDER SECRETS

GREAT ENERGY

Kelly says: 'People might think it's crazy, but I am a firm believer in the importance of good energy in a home. My shamanic energy consultant, Sofia Stainton, helped me enormously when I moved into my apartment. To begin with, I felt very uncomfortable there and it seemed as though there were endless building problems, that things never ran smoothly. I began to worry I had bought a monster. Here is what Sofia explained.'

'Kelly's apartment is part of an old school, but when buildings undergo a change of use the energy can become very confused. It is a very big, powerful space, so it was important to make sure that the energy could flow smoothly. Being close to a railway line, it also suffers from a certain amount of geopathic stress.

On the positive side, it had once been a science laboratory, so it had good connotations with invention and learning. Being part of a girls' school, it also had a natural affinity with things female. What we had to do was direct the energy better and unblock it where it had become stuck.

That might sound cranky, but to understand this better you have to accept the premise that everything – including us – is made of energy. Energy is circulating through your home all the time, even if you cannot see it. In acupuncture, needles are used to release blocked energy in the body. What I do is unblock energy within the home, a form of earth acupuncture, using all manner of things such as crystals, colour, candles and music. As an example, one thing I advised Kelly was that she use metal balls at the kitchen end of the main room, to reflect energy back into the house. She achieved this perfectly by hanging chainmail at the windows – hundreds and hundreds of small metal balls (see left). Once we had finished working on the house, not only did the atmosphere feel completely different, but all the building work began to flow easily. It is still a big field of energy that not everyone would be able to hold, but for Kelly it now feels as a home should.'
Sofia Stainton

THIS PAGE *This light, summery room, designed with symmetry and harmony, is dedicated to the owners' passion for orchids. Silk lanterns hung above these oriental blooms complement their exotic beauty.*

Lighting

Functional, atmospheric and sculptural, lighting has become one of the most dynamic design ingredients of the era.

ABOVE *Chandeliers are popular because they add a decorative layer to the lighting scheme. Here a contemporary one of twisted metal, 'Oval Sphere' by Brandvan Egmond, is placed over the runner on a black stained table.*

RIGHT *Designed by John Wigmore of Wigmore Lighting Designs, this dramatic light has been created to frame the mirror stretching from wall to wall. A central pendant adds ambient light.*

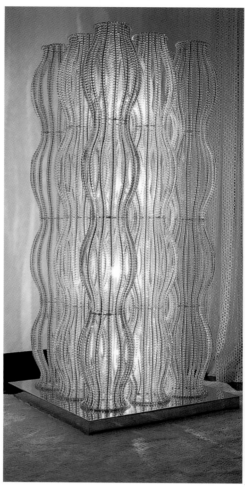

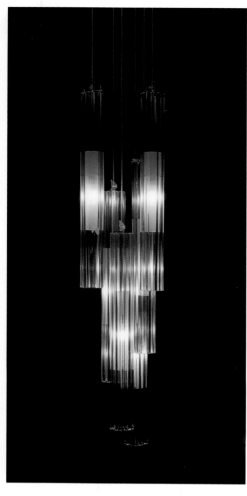

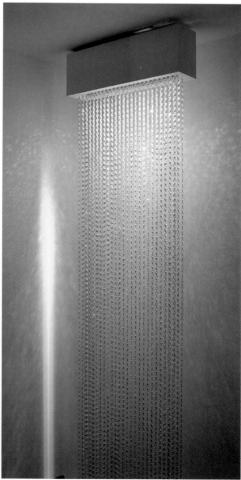

TOP FAR LEFT *Increasingly, lights are used as sculpture. The curvy form of Mathieu Lustrerie's crystal Lalique-style lamp contrasts with the linear design of the rest of the room's scheme.*

TOP LEFT *Single central pendant lights have fallen from favour, but ones that are targeted on specific corners within a room can be highly effective, as with these glass cylinders from Solzi Luce hung at each side of a bed.*

BELOW FAR LEFT *This incredible light sculpture, with its organic lacquered base and multi-armed lamps, is by David Gill. It not only casts illumination, but is also a striking focal point.*

BELOW LEFT *This Swarovski crystal pendant light seems to send sparkling illumination flooding down the wall like water.*

OPPOSITE TOP LEFT *Table lamps are practical for reading and are often objects of interest and elegance in their own right – the chrome rings and silk shade of this lamp from Porta Romana strike a note of quiet glamour.*

OPPOSITE TOP RIGHT *A sculptural crystal and polished nickel floor lamp by Mathieu Lustrerie harmonizes beautifully with the sweeping lines of this architect-designed house, echoing the muted colours of stone and the Mies Van Der Rohe 'Barcelona' chairs. The 'Tabou' table was designed by Eric Schmitt for Christian Liaigre.*

OPPOSITE BOTTOM RIGHT *Traditional wall lamps have been given a contemporary twist with slender nickel arms and chains of crystal. When lit, they cast intriguing shadows onto the textured plastered wall behind.*

KELLY SAYS

When you are in a hotel, restaurant or private home that makes you feel especially comfortable, note how it is lit and see whether you can take any ideas from it.

PROFESSIONAL LIGHTING

Lighting for me is a real passion – it is about achieving balance and creating a feel-good quality in each particular setting. I think of myself as painting with light. Working with Kelly enables me to stretch my creativity to the outer limits because her commissions are always so challenging and visually stimulating.

I am always looking for ways to create different effects that work for all types of budgets, both large and small. The secret of good lighting is to have three or four circuits in each room. A standard requirement would be a 5 amp circuit for table lamps, floor lamps and task lighting; recess lighting to highlight artwork or *objets d'art*; accent lighting; possible wall light points for uplighters or sconces for ambient lighting; and perhaps a circuit for lighting any fitted furniture or interesting corners or alcoves to add some drama. Dimmers are a must so that you can change the look of the room by raising or lowering light levels and create different moods for different occasions.

If your budget permits, you can have a pre-set system that will allow you to select different scenes at the touch of a button. The scenes can be set to fade in and out. Pre-set systems enable you to create different scenes for different times of the day for functional use and entertaining. They are more expensive, but if they fit into your overall budget they are worth it. Thanks to technology and people being more aware of the need for good lighting, the systems are increasingly more accessible pricewise.

As soon as you have determined your furniture layout, it is important to allow for floor sockets for table lamps and freestanding floor lamps. You have to be careful that you position them correctly, as they will need to be cut into the flooring. Once they are in place, you cannot decide to change your furniture layout entirely.

I would also advise having points for wall lights installed, even if, at this stage, you decide not to use them. You can always blank them off or hide them under pictures for now, but it means that you have the option in the future. It is better to prepare for all eventualities where lighting is concerned.

It is my job to design a lighting scheme that will ensure the lighting will fall in the right place – with points for task lighting, table lamps and so on. My job is obviously easier when Kelly is designing from scratch, as I can make sure there are enough circuits in each room and that all the points are precisely where they should be. However, there are tricks I use when Kelly is decorating an existing scheme that does not allow for the upheaval of rewiring. In my experience, there are always a few ways of cleverly concealing cables to feed any circuits that may be required, as there is a lot of lighting available off the shelf that can be used. An architectural tube sitting on top of an armoire or bookcase can give a fabulous effect and if you have a local 5 amp point, you can simply plug your light source in, run a flex up behind the piece of furniture and switch on. I have also camouflaged cables behind screeens, mirrors and artwork.

Rob Clift

OPPOSITE *In my own hall I wanted low-level light washing over the dark wood floor beneath the 'Velin' banquettes by Christian Liaigre. Rob Clift designed a light baffle to replace the skirting board, but retained recessed lights in the ceiling to light the artwork by Peter Beard.*

TOP RIGHT *Functional light is important in bathrooms but can be rather unflattering.*

Here low-voltage recessed lights positioned in the ceiling wash light onto the basin, while frosted-glass diffusers set into the mirror soften their effect.

RIGHT *This vanity mirror has three sections with an integral tungsten lightbox between each one, providing the perfect light for applying make-up. Concealed low-voltage cabinet lights wash light onto the floor.*

In the Mood – Lighting

THE CHALLENGE: To create a visually stunning multifunctional space in a purpose-built apartment.

THE SOLUTION: To use lighting to zone different areas and to bring out the beauty of texture and colours within the scheme.

This was a new development that had no original features, so I had to create something more out of it than already existed. My brief was to design a truly multifunctional space that all the family could share, and also to find ways of imbuing the apartment with character. This was made easier by the clients' own collection of striking contemporary photographic art, and also by the installation of a really superlative lighting scheme.

The main living space had to incorporate seating with a home cinema, dining table, study area and bar. As the plan on page 30

KEY CONSIDERATIONS

Achieving well-designed multifunctionality – the main living space also had to encompass a dining area, home cinema, bar and study.

Using lighting to enhance each zone and visually separate it from the others.

Introducing character and visual interest to a modern apartment.

Making the most of the client's stunning collection of contemporary art.

Installing a lighting system that could be set to create different moods within the same room.

Building maximum flexibility into the lighting scheme, so that pieces of furniture or pictures could be moved around or changed in the future and still be well lit.

Using fabulous combinations of textures to create a really luxurious feel.

CIRCUIT 1 *Low-voltage recessed directional downlighters to wash onto artwork, to include one set in fitted unit for artwork and one positioned over coffee table.*

CIRCUIT 2 *Low-voltage recess lights to wash onto seating area.*

CIRCUIT 3 *5 amp points for table and floor lamps.*

CIRCUIT 4 *Feature chandelier over dining table.*

CIRCUIT 5 *Rectangular suspended shade above writing table in window recess.*

CIRCUIT 6 *Low-voltage recess lights to wash onto widow treatments/blinds.*

CIRCUIT 7 *Low-voltage recessed floor lights set into floor to uplight screen.*

CIRCUIT 8 *Low-voltage low-level floor washers to gently wash light onto floor finish.*

CIRCUIT 9 *Integral low-voltage lighting to highlight objects in bespoke wall unit.*

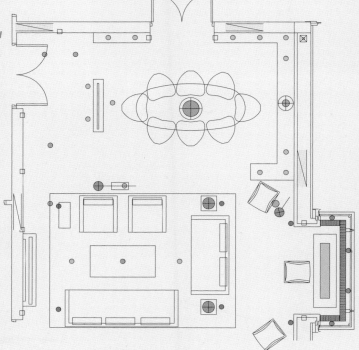

OPPOSITE *The main living area, shown here by day, has to achieve several functions – comfy seating, with 'Mousson' sofas and armchairs by Christian Liaigre, dining room, study, bar and home cinema. Photographic art by Vanessa Beecroft has been positioned for maximum visual impact. A wealth of different textures have been used to give each zone its own identity within the space.*

ABOVE *At night the room takes on a new look, with lighting designed to illuminate certain areas, from the faux candles in the fireplace to the crystal chandelier by Mark Brazier-Jones. Different lighting 'scenes' can be created at the touch of a button. The 'CL4' reading light is by Christian Liaigre and the table lamp is by Mathieu Lustrerie.*

LEFT *A simplified version of lighting consultant Rob Clift's lighting scheme for the same room. The highlighted areas show some of the circuits in place – for the chandelier, table lamps, uplighters and downlighters (see key). A pre-set dimming system allows these to be faded in and out.*

shows, this was quite a tall order even for such a large room. What was crucial was to find ways of zoning off the different areas as and when they were needed, so the space never felt cramped or cluttered. Once I had solved the challenge of the furniture layout and numbered where each piece of artwork would go, I handed over the plans to Rob Clift. He then came up with a lighting scheme that used a great number of different circuits: one for table lamps placed centrally in the room; one for table lamps positioned against the walls; one for the crystal chandelier above the dining table; one for the recessed uplighters in the specially commissioned screen; one for the faux candles within the fireplace; one for low-level floor washers; one for recessed downlighters in the bookcase and others positioned to light particular pieces of art. Some of these circuits were then split, so that not everything on the same circuit had to be lit at once. In addition, the pre-set dimmer system allows the client to alter the mood by dropping individual lamps to, say, 30 per cent of their brightness.

The whole apartment has benefited from this attention to detail where lighting is concerned, whether it is the way that the eelskin headboard in the master bedroom is illuminated to accentuate texture or the Hollywood-style vanity unit that provides the perfect light for applying make-up. Rob has considered each texture I have

used – from the silver leaf on the walls in the living room to the shagreen inlay of the bedside tables – and made sure the lighting is appropriate to bring out the beauty in each.

The electrical planning this needs might sound unduly complicated, but the result is stunning. The system that Rob installed also allows the client to pre-set certain 'scenes', so they can have the perfect light for dining, reading or watching a film by at the touch of a button. Not only has the lighting meant that many different looks can be created in one space, according to the function of the moment, but it has also engendered a real feel-good factor and enhanced every aspect of the interior design.

OPPOSITE TOP *Small 12 volt starlighters are recessed into the mirror on the vanity unit adjacent to the master bedroom (opposite bottom left), controlled by a pre-set system. At full power they provide a bright light for applying make-up, but when dimmed they give a soft and sexy glow.*

OPPOSITE BOTTOM LEFT *The master bedroom by day: I layered up luxurious textures, such as eelskin on the bedhead and a tactile mix of velvet, silk and fur for the bed itself. A wall of specialist plaster behind the bed provides the perfect backdrop for the photographic artwork by Desiree Dolron.*

OPPOSITE BOTTOM RIGHT *Lighting has been positioned to enhance the various textures in the bedroom. Light sources are placed close to the artwork on the false partition, so that they send out arcs of light that wash down the art and onto the bedhead. Bedside lights for reading are on a separate circuit.*

ABOVE *This wooden screen separates the dining area within the main room from the door into the hall. Rather than light it with uplighters placed in the floor, Rob Clift had recessed uplighters put into the plinth. Small recessed integral downlighters set into the bookcase illuminate the displays.*

Visual impact

Once the scheme is finished, it is the art and other objects you add that express your personality and wit.

STAR PIECES There is no better way of expressing your personality in the home than through what you hang on your walls or choose to display. It takes time to build up a collection of art, but it is well worth doing because it gives you such pleasure. If you can put money aside for this purpose, buy one sensational picture that you really love, rather than six mediocre ones. See it as a chance to express yourself, not simply to fill up the walls.

When it comes to art, there are essentially two directions to take: if you have an exceptionally great collection, then you need to use the colours and textures in the room as a backdrop to this. In other words, look to draw the eye to the art rather than to the walls. If, however, you simply want to hang something on the walls that fits with the general style of the room, then you might

OPPOSITE *Halls and landings can make perfect gallery spaces for wall-hung art, sculpture or star pieces of furniture. This egg-like chest from David Gill, designed by Garouste & Bonetti and made of oak silver-plated in bronze, is juxtaposed with work by Icelandic Pop artist Erro.*

RIGHT *A piece of photographic artwork by Peter Beard based on African landscape has inspired the juxtaposition of this primitive-looking wooden vessel from Concho Bay. The simple fluid lines of Christain Liaigre's 'Saline' daybed placed below punctuate the space between the two.*

BELOW *A neutral scheme provides the best backdrop for art with strong colours and forms. This striking example of geometric abstract art by French-Hungarian Op artist Vasarely pulls the eye towards it.*

do better to look for artwork that suits the general ambience – black-and-white photography, for example, is a good choice and is becoming increasingly collectible. Try to avoid mixing different styles of art together, unless you are very confident in what you are doing. Traditional watercolour landscapes, for instance, are not the obvious companions for modern abstracts.

If you wish to anchor a collection of paintings or photographs together on a wall, unifying the framing is an effective way to achieve this. Using white mounts with all white or all black frames is an easy way of making a disparate collection into a striking group. If you follow this route, hang all the pictures together on one wall rather than scattering them around a room.

KELLY SAYS

Art must be hung at the right height – people constantly hang their pictures too high. You should be able to look at a painting without tilting your head upwards.

In terms of star pieces, now that great designs are readily available on the high street, it has become even more important to find individual ways to make a style statement in your home. As with fashion, the trick is to mix designer, high street and vintage in order to achieve a truly personal look. I have always loved to introduce antique pieces into my schemes, but this is something I now do more and more. I have also become excited by quirky vintage designs, which are not in themselves of great monetary value but which have a wit and vitality that really bring a room alive. I am particularly keen on using vintage lamps – in addition to providing another layer of light, they come in fantastic forms and textures that look wonderful juxtaposed with cool modern objects.

There is a skill to combining pieces of very different provenance, though, so my advice would be not to buy too much vintage if this is a departure from your usual style. Choose things that you truly love, not ones that you contrive to make work. Compare and contrast are the key words. You either need to make a visual link between objects, such as using an elaborate nineteenth-century French chandelier in pink glass above an ultra-modern pink lacquer table; or you need to spark a reaction by juxtaposing something like a curved Art Deco lamp against a hard-edged black walnut and steel desk. Using vintage pieces successfully is all about creating a *frisson*, a slight jarring on the senses – as though you have finished a jigsaw puzzle and then removed a couple of pieces at random, so that it is no longer perfect.

Remember that tastes change, so never feel that once in place artworks cannot be replaced or moved to a different part of the house. One of the quickest ways of injecting a home with new vitality is to look at the paintings or objects displayed with a fresh eye and determine to reposition them. Sometimes an item that has been sidelined will come centre stage again.

DISPLAY

DISPLAY The skill of successful display is knowing how to set off an individual object or a collection to best effect. It centres on two different approaches. The first is about making the most of something that is beautiful in its own right. The second is about making a visual statement by doing something remarkable with an object that is not in itself valuable or eye-catching.

You may wish to house a treasured collection in a piece of furniture that will become a focal point within a room. Floating shelves are also an effective display area. Lighting is important, but make sure you don't overilluminate the area; incorporating lighting underneath shelves gives an atmospheric glow, while fibre optics are an excellent way of adding interest to displays.

If it is individual artefacts that you wish to display, think carefully about where to place them for maximum effect. Don't crowd something you wish to be noticed – leaving enough space around an object makes all the difference.

You can make a display from almost anything. One signature look of mine is to use rows of glass goldfish bowls with either white sand and coral, or coils of white rope. Repetition is the key: if you put enough like objects together, they take on an impact that is much greater than their individual parts.

You must be disciplined. Overdo any display and the result will look cluttered rather than smart. Achieve balance either through grouping identically sized and shaped objects, or by choosing items of different scales and forms that complement each other. A bookcase, for example, may be used either to house only books or to mix books with photo frames, sculpture and magazines.

Finally, don't let displays remain static for too long. You can transform the look and feel of a space by ringing the changes every six months or so. Simply pack up one collection of objects and take another out of storage – it is really fun to discover things all over again and feel inspired to display them in a new way.

OPPOSITE LEFT *When art and pieces of furniture are juxtaposed with each other, make sure the two work together in harmony. Here a silver gelatin print, (Untitled) Mirror Series, by contemporary French artist Valerie Belin is hung above a dark stained cabinet.*

OPPOSITE CENTRE *Collections need not be displayed in an obvious way. This stack of antique blue-and-white plates placed on a simple antique Chinese table creates a pleasing still life in a sumptuous dining room.*

OPPOSITE RIGHT *A figurative sculpture by Toutain is placed on a plinth at the foot of this boldly sweeping staircase in stained oak, accentuating its sense of movement and flow.*

ABOVE *Balance is key when it comes to display. This can be achieved through grouping objects of an identical size and shape together, but placing them in the context of an object of a different scale, such as these antique Chinese Ming dynasty terracotta figurines on a mantelpiece.*

RIGHT *Built-in shelves are the ideal setting for an eclectic group of objects, such as photographs, vases, pots and candles. Change the look and feel of a space by rearranging the display twice a year or so.*

OPPOSITE *These lacquered cupboard doors have become part of the composition of a dining room, because carefully positioned downlighters not only highlight the surface of individual objects, but also wash light and shadow over the furniture itself.*

ABOVE *Think about what colour to use when you are creating a backdrop for an eclectic display. Here shelves with dividers, which have been stained black, transform this individual arrangement of books, objects and vases by Anna Torfs into a harmonious still life.*

ABOVE RIGHT *Dining rooms are the perfect place in which to house collections, for both beauty and interest. Here vellum books, antique china and Tang dynasty horses make an elegant display and an interesting conversation piece within an illuminated bookcase in front of a table by David Linley.*

KELLY SAYS

If you see something you love that won't break the bank, buy a collection of them – a group has such impact compared with one item.

KELLY'S INSIDER SECRETS

Wherever you want a display, begin by taking everything away.

Edit down the items you wish to display and store the rest away.

Too much symmetry can look dead and flat. Find your centre then radiate out with a balanced arrangement of objects.

Don't take the most obvious approach – overlapping a collection of photographs of different sizes will look more interesting than lining up uniform-sized ones along a shelf.

Experiment with the juxtaposition of form, texture and colour in your chosen group of objects.

Make sure you connect the display to the rest of the scheme, perhaps through an accent of colour.

Once you have finished arranging your objects or pictures, go and have a cup of coffee, then look at the display again with a fresh eye. There are often improvements to be made.

Take it all away and begin again every few months.

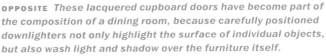

Creating theatre

THE CHALLENGE: To take a purpose-built modern apartment and create an interior that would provide a glamorous backdrop to the client's superb collection of art and *objets d'art*.

THE SOLUTION: To keep the schemes as pure and simple as possible in order to draw the eye to the collection of bold statement pieces on display.

This is a purpose-built apartment, which has been elevated to a gallery-style space by the clients' incredible collection of art, sculpture and furniture. Some of the pieces were commissioned specially to fit certain spaces, but a collection this good would look sensational almost no matter how it was laid out.

As a designer, what I had to do was make sure that the decorative schemes never fought for attention with the art, but provided a clean, calm backdrop that allowed each piece to speak for itself. The clients also wanted their home to be intensely glamorous, so the key lay in building up wonderfully luxurious textures, such as the shag-pile carpet of pure silk and the lighting sculptures made of Swarovski crystal. The aim was to feed the senses with an intense experience of different textures, atmospheric lighting and unexpected juxtapositions of form.

There also had to be an energetic flow from room to room, so I kept the interior very minimalist, with simple but striking lines of black and white throughout. With so many strong pieces, it was important that each one be set in its own space, so that the eye never felt confused but could take in all there is to see.

In effect, a house like this is all about creating a sense of theatre. Internal architecture, such as the black stained doorframes, creates a stage full of the promise of drama. As with any theatre, lighting is also key – both in terms of showing off star pieces to their best effect, but also in making a statement itself through sculptural pieces of decorative lighting. You also have to consider the views from room to room, and in particular the first impressions you create. This is the kind of space where you should feel your heart beating a little faster as you walk through the door.

KEY CONSIDERATIONS

Creating the perfect backdrop for the client's collection of art and statement pieces.

Deciding where in the home each piece should be displayed to its best advantage.

Injecting the apartment with a sense of drama and glamour.

Ensuring it was lit to best effect.

Mixing in luxurious layers of texture.

Keeping the interior scheme essentially monochromatic throughout.

Playing with the form of furniture, sculpture and other objects to provide further levels of interest and excitement.

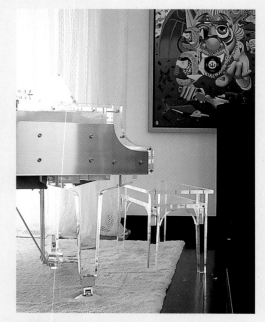

TOP *Pieces of furniture can be chosen for their sculptural quality and the way in which they interreact with one another. One of the star pieces in this living room is the Perspex piano, one of only a handful made. Rather than being positioned centrally in the room, it has been placed in one of the corners where, in front of the artwork by Chamizo, it draws the eye. Lighting has been used to highlight its reflective quality.*

ABOVE *This mosaic mirror by Davide Medri adds a boldly glamorous touch that is heightened by the purity of white walls and dark stained wood. Reflected in it is a line of panelled glass doors, which draw the eye to vistas beyond.*

OPPOSITE *These opulent twists of crystal are lighting sculptures by Michael Anastassiades for Swarovski, commissioned for the client. Through the window behind is a double-height wall of water (see page 115), which makes a striking backdrop to their form and sparkle.*

ROOM BOARD *In a room that is all about glamour and theatre, form and texture are key. The right-hand side of the room board shows a palette of mainly pale shades in touchy-feely materials. A dark wood finish (22) on the floor is the base for the luxurious silk rug (23). Sheer curtains in parachute silk (10) hung from nickel-plated poles (21) blend with the Orchid paint (8) on the walls. This creates a calm shell in which to display key pieces such as the antique carved silver sofa (11), crystal lamp by Mathieu Lustrerie (1 and 12), rare Perspex piano (14) and 'Ghost' chair by Fiam (19). The Christian Liaigre ottoman (7) is upholstered in caramel leather (15), while cream leather (5) has been used for the silver sofa (11). The contemporary sofa (3) and unusual chairs by India Mahdavi (20) fit perfectly with these bold forms. Boiled-wool cushions (9) have been banded in contrasting linen (16 and 18) or adorned with mother-of-pearl buttons (4). Side tables with silver trays by Holly Hunt (2) and white lacquered shelving (17) add more layers of texture. The drum stool (6) and elegant 'Chantecaille' floor lamp by Christian Liaigre (13) continue the play with form.*

Piano, see p136 top & opposite bottom left

Seating arrangement of armchairs, side tables and lamp, see opposite bottom left

Antique sofa with two side tables, see opposite top & bottom right

Sofa

Coffee table

Stairs to hallway, see opposite

Glass chair, see opposite, opposite bottom right & p91 bottom

Living area, see opposite bottom right

Sofa

Crystal floor lamp, see p120 top left

ABOVE *The floor plan of the living room shows how wide stairs lead into it, creating a sense of theatre from the beginning. The furniture is the star, from the Perspex piano in one corner to the antique silver sofa in the centre. This is the pivot around which the two sitting areas are positioned, balancing each half of the room.*

OPPOSITE BOTTOM LEFT *The fabulous sculptural shape of India Mahdavi's semicircular seats is a focal point in the symmetrically arranged living area. Their curved form plays against the linear structure of the chairs placed opposite and the tall floor lamp by Christian Liaigre. The window is flanked by two artworks by Chamizo.*

OPPOSITE BOTTOM RIGHT *The living room is a confidently eclectic mix of antique and modern, quiet and bold, transparent and dense, simple and ornate – all set against the yin and yang of a monochromatic decorative scheme. The artwork behind the sofa is by Antonio Segui.*

In the Mood – Art

THE CHALLENGE: To take an apartment in a new development and transform it into a comfortable family home that would also be a backdrop for the clients' collection of contemporary art.
THE SOLUTION: To create vistas within the apartment where individual pieces of art could be enjoyed to best advantage.

This is the same home as that shown on pages 30–1 and 126–9. My clients had bought this brand-new purpose-built apartment, which was, in effect, a blank canvas upon which I could work. Their brief to me was to transform it into a family home full of personality and interest. They have a keen interest in contemporary art, so it was important to make sure their collection was shown off to good effect, while making sure it was also well assimilated into what is essentially a practical family space.

If the art were to be shown to maximum effect, I first had to find ways of creating interesting vistas for it. I began by tackling the lack of original features through a total redesign of the internal architecture. The hall, for example, was originally lined with a busy wall of unprepossessing doors.

Replacing these with sliding panels of leather not only created a sense of drama, but also added a note of mystery – were these doors or not?

In the master bedroom I replaced the ubiquitous fitted wardrobes with decorative Versailles-inspired panelling in a painted blue finish – for me, this really was stepping out of my box. Usually I keep internal cabinetry very simple and modern, and

OPPOSITE *A 'wrapped' yellow velvet chair provides a dramatic accent of colour in the reading corner of the living room, with an artwork by Luis Tomasello displayed on the wall behind. The floor-to-ceiling bookcase makes a further point of interest; its linear shape contrasts with the curves of the chair.*

ABOVE *In the hall, doors were replaced with leather-panelled screens that slide open and closed. The lightboxes by Hans Op De Beeck, Determination (13) (left) and Determination (2) (right) are juxtaposed with Chinese chairs and an antique chiffonier.*

KEY CONSIDERATIONS

Adding character to a modern apartment.

Rethinking all the internal architecture, doors in particular.

Displaying the clients' art to best effect.

Using accents of colour for additional interest.

Playing with the forms of furniture – curved against linear.

rarely does blue make it onto one of my room boards. However, the clients loved it and it is now one of my favourite rooms.

The aim was to achieve a look that was as far removed from the original new-build as possible. It was also important to create an interesting backdrop where art could be enjoyed to optimum advantage. Interestingly, we did not always end up hanging certain pictures where we had first envisaged them. Once the scheme was finished, the clients and I had enormous fun trying out different artwork in different places – sometimes being swayed by the power of an image and sometimes simply by the colours within.

In many ways, the old maxim 'less is more' is a good one to bear in mind. With artwork as strong as this, it would be a mistake to have too much hung too close together. Some things worked naturally as a pair, such as the 'lightbox' art in the hall or the abstracts around the informal seating area, but others – such as the remarkable artwork of the child that is hung in the kitchen – need to be seen in isolation as they have even more impact.

Whereas in some houses it makes sense to use a simple monochromatic scheme to create a gallery-style effect (as in the apartment shown on pages 136–9), here I wanted to do the opposite and to use layers and layers of texture to provide a feeling of warmth and comfort. The art is an integral feature of this home, but I did not want it to dominate entirely. The skill lay in making it sit happily within a space that was first and foremost a family home.

ABOVE RIGHT *This incredible gelatine silver collection print by Jean Baptiste Huynh is the star piece when looking from the dining area through to the kitchen – one sensational image is enough to create impact.*

RIGHT *Desiree Dolron's photographic artwork above the master bed has been chosen mainly for its soft colours, which blend beautifully with the painted Versailles-inspired panelling.*

OPPOSITE *A pair of diptique abstract paintings by Pia Fries are the focal point in this informal seating area, part of the main living room. Flowers were chosen to accent the colours.*

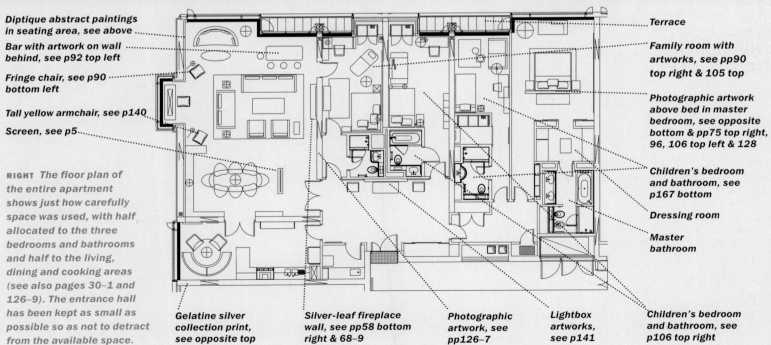

Diptique abstract paintings in seating area, see above

Bar with artwork on wall behind, see p92 top left

Fringe chair, see p90 bottom left

Tall yellow armchair, see p140

Screen, see p5

RIGHT *The floor plan of the entire apartment shows just how carefully space was used, with half allocated to the three bedrooms and bathrooms and half to the living, dining and cooking areas (see also pages 30–1 and 126–9). The entrance hall has been kept as small as possible so as not to detract from the available space.*

Terrace

Family room with artworks, see pp90 top right & 105 top

Photographic artwork above bed in master bedroom, see opposite bottom & pp75 top right, 96, 106 top left & 128

Children's bedroom and bathroom, see p167 bottom

Dressing room

Master bathroom

Gelatine silver collection print, see opposite top

Silver-leaf fireplace wall, see pp58 bottom right & 68–9

Photographic artwork, see pp126–7

Lightbox artworks, see p141

Children's bedroom and bathroom, see p106 top right

ABOVE *Double-height double doors make an impressive statement in my own apartment, taking the eye from the bedroom across the hall to the living room beyond, with the Christian Liaigre sofa and India Mahdavi lamp.*

ROOM BY ROOM OVERVIEW

The aim of good design is to achieve a sense of flow from room to room, so that nothing jars or strikes a discordant note. Ideally, you should consider every room equally and tackle the project as a whole, but time and budget may not allow this. My advice is to tackle the design of every room, even if you can't put it all into practice at once. You will benefit from having a complete blueprint to refer to when the time comes.

Arriving and travelling through

Creating a good first impression is the aim of the hall, not just for the benefit of guests but for you, too.

We all live in a world that at times feels dangerous, pressured and challenging. Your home is the place where you feel safe and free to be yourself. That feeling should kick in the moment you turn the key in the lock and step through your own front door. If you can't relax when you come home, where can you relax?

There is a lot written about first impressions when it comes to halls, but what people forget is that it isn't just the first impression on a visitor that counts, but the one on you, too. The sense of smell is one that we consistently underrate, but in fact smell is highly evocative. Everyone's home smells different – you want yours to smell exactly as you like it to and for that to be something you notice when you walk in, even if this is at quite a subliminal level. It is all part of the coming-home experience.

When designing a hall, begin by solving the practical decisions: where are coats to be hung and umbrellas stored? Is there a place for keys, gloves or dog leads? Do you need space for a pushchair or a bike? Lighting is important, not only to create atmosphere and comfort when you arrive in the dark, but also to make visitors feel safe when they are waiting to be let in. Low-level floor lights look fabulous in halls and on stairs, and are also a safety feature.

You then need to come up with a way of giving your hall panache. This should start on the external side of the front door. Find a way of making yours individual – through colour, door furniture, size or any other means. From the moment someone walks through that door, they should find themselves in a place that accurately represents you. The hall should embody the signature of your home, and there should be a feeling that all other rooms flow from this one point. Don't jar the effect by changing design direction when you go from the hall into the living room or kitchen.

ABOVE RIGHT *Entrances benefit from a sense of theatre and drama. Here tall double doors open to a runner of black wood on a polished stone floor, which has the effect of pulling the eye forwards to the sofa by Andrée Putman (for Ralph Pucci).*

RIGHT *If a hall is large enough, it can be used as a room in its own right. This magnificent double-height space flooded with natural light makes an additional seating area, with 'Atlantide' floor lamps by Christian Liaigre positioned beside the sofas for reading at night.*

OPPOSITE *Large halls make perfect gallery spaces, not just for paintings but for three-dimensional objects, too. Here a Giacometti original is placed next to a sculptural high-backed chair upholstered in crushed velvet.*

Think about depth and height. Stairs lead the eye upwards, so accentuate this by encouraging the eye to sweep vertically by drawing it to features such as a large-scale mirror, an artwork or a magnificent chandelier. Super-tall internal doors give a sense of grandeur and excitement. You can introduce interest to the floor by creating a runner effect, such as dark wood inset on pale stone. The slimmer the runner is, the more depth it gives to a room. A wide runner will make the space feel cosier and more intimate.

You can't consider the hall in isolation from stairs, landings or other connecting areas. These are spaces in which people are on the move, so it is important to keep that feeling of flow by choosing colours that don't shout for attention. Once the initial 'wow' reaction has been established, there should be a sense of drawing the visitor in deeper.

Halls are all about anticipation of what is to follow. Make yours as visually exciting as you can. Use a focal piece of furniture chosen for its interesting form, find space for an exuberant flower arrangement or make a bold display of collected objects – add an inviting scent, as I mentioned, and you set the scene for sensory delight. The hall is the beginning of a journey through your home, so do all you can to make it an enjoyable one.

BELOW LEFT *In a chalet designed for comfort and relaxation, skis and poles are hung on the wall both for practicality and decoration.*

BELOW *In my own apartment the first vista when walking up the stairs is of a pair of fabulous antique mirrors.*

RIGHT *The curved brick wall separating this hallway from the cloakroom emphasizes this house's relationship with its exterior.*

KELLY SAYS

Halls are all about anticipation. You want yours to engender the same excitement as when you walk into a fabulous party – it is all about the unexpected.

Friends and family

Living rooms should be welcoming, imbuing those who use them with a feeling of warmth, comfort and deep relaxation.

A generation ago, the living room or drawing room was often described as 'a place for best', meaning it was set apart from the everyday activity of the rest of the house, a dignified sanctuary in which honoured guests were entertained. Happily, contemporary living means this kind of stuffy formality is largely a thing of the past. When it comes to designing a living room, however, the first question must always be: is this the place in which you will spend time with friends or relax with family – or is that now more likely to happen in the kitchen area? If so, when is this room going to be used and by whom?

There are practical reasons why you have to tackle the question of whether a living room is going to be a family place or a more adult one – if it is the former, you might like to have washable loose covers on sofas, for example, and floors that can withstand muddy trainers. However, my message is: if you do decide to have a dedicated living room, don't decorate it in such a way that it is rarely filled with people. You don't want a return to the days of having a 'best' room.

In fact, if space permits, most people now like to have two living areas – a relaxed family snug for watching television or listening to music and a slightly more elegant one for entertaining guests. However, I am on a mission to bring the television into all living areas. The fact is that if you put a television into a room, that room immediately becomes more friendly. Rooms without televisions are often not used enough, because people gravitate towards the place where the television is. Gone are the days when we had to feel embarrassed by the television, continually looking for ways to camouflage it into the rest of the room. It is possible today to buy ones that are really attractive pieces of design in their own right. Why hide them away? My pet hate of the moment is the trend to use fake pieces of art to cover up televisions. Don't entertain such an idea.

As I have mentioned, when choosing furniture, comfort should always be the driving word. You simply cannot buy an item as important as a sofa or armchair by looking at catalogues or browsing on the Internet; you need to try things out for yourself. You don't

want a sofa that just looks good; you want one that makes you feel instantly relaxed and at ease. There is nothing more likely to make a guest feel uncomfortable than to be perched on the edge of a chair with their feet barely touching the ground, so choose designs that engender a more welcoming feel. You also need to think about how to lay out the furniture. I use a lot of backless and sideless seats in my schemes, because they introduce an informal touch to otherwise formal seating. They are also a great way to connect different areas of a living room, because they allow views from one to the other. For me, they are often the final vital pieces in the furniture jigsaw.

Do think about whether you want only one sitting area – usually grouped around the fireplace and television – or whether you have sufficient room to introduce a second or even a third. Different parts of a room offer different views and it can be satisfying to have a special place for reading, for example, perhaps looking out of the window onto the garden; or to have a couple of chairs set up for playing cards, backgammon or chess. If you design a living room with more than one activity in mind, it is far more likely to be used on a regular basis. Also, remember that fireplaces, like televisions, bring a feeling of comfort to a room. If you have one, then make sure it can be used – fires create warmth in every sense of the word.

Planning the furniture layout will also determine where the lighting is to be located. If you want to read, you don't want a light positioned directly over your head because you will be in your own shadow. The light needs to fall directly on the page, not on you. The

LEFT *In a multifunctional open-plan living area, it makes sense to have more than one seating area. Christian Liaigre's 'Mousson' sofas and armchairs are arranged centrally in the room round a coffee table, but a smaller reading corner, with curved sofa by Interior Craft, has also been created in front of the window.*

BELOW *There has never been a better time to mix old and new furniture. These two old-fashioned wing armchairs have been given a new lease of life by re-covering, enabling them to blend perfectly with more contemporary sofas. On the table is a glass sculpture by Amanda Brisbane and bowls by McCollin Bryan.*

LEFT *Rich, tactile textures, such as leather, sheepskin, suede and velvet, have been used to build up layers of warmth and character in this cosy mountain chalet. Built-in book shelves at the far end of the room are an interesting focal point.*

OPPOSITE TOP *In this kitchen-cum-family space, the television has been integrated into a piece of custom-made furniture, placed centrally, which visually divides the area in half. Positioned on a pivot, it can be watched from either end of the room.*

OPPOSITE BOTTOM RIGHT *This is another view of the room shown above, this time looking towards the seating end. The single armchair placed in front of the floor-to-ceiling window is needed to balance the furniture layout, because it pulls the eye around the television to the living space beyond.*

OPPOSITE BOTTOM LEFT *Home cinema areas are the trend in many contemporary homes, particularly in ones where there is more than one living space. Sleek and unobtrusive, wall-mounted screens are an elegant solution to the question of where to put the television, with unsightly wires hidden from view.*

more circuits you have in a living room, the more you can vary the effect of different lamps, wall sconces and recessed spotlights, and so create different ambiences.

Storage also needs careful consideration. This is a room for relaxing and few things are more unrelaxing than mess and clutter. The only way to avoid it is to list every item that needs to be kept here, such as DVDs or newspapers, and to devise an appropriate way of storing it. Custom-made cabinets that include both open and closed storage are ideal, as you can hide unsightly items away while drawing the eye to carefully edited displays.

Finally, do allow yourself and others to really live here. I like to come home to a place that looks pristine and perfect, but of course it doesn't look like that the next morning. Homes are not for show. They are for letting your hair down in and really enjoying.

KELLY SAYS

Televisions are not something to be ashamed of – buy a design you really like, sit back and enjoy.

MAKING THE MOST OF YOUR LIVING ROOM

Ask yourself who is going to use this room, what activities they will they do here and at what times of the day.

Decide how you are going to integrate audiovisual systems.

Think about the focal point of the room – if there is no fireplace, you need to give it another centre.

Make sure you have flexible, versatile lighting that is both comfortable when you want to rest and well positioned for activities such as reading.

Choose types of seating that will suit every member of the family.

Experiment with how furniture should best be laid out and whether there is flexibility for when the occasion demands.

Take into account how easy your finished scheme will be to maintain.

Provide adequate storage – both closed and open – for all types of item that need to be kept close at hand – from hi-fis and other media equipment to DVDs, CDs, magazines and books.

Quiet corners

A working area within the home needs a gentle touch if it is to blend into its surroundings.

Perhaps the most significant change in the way we live now compared with 20 years ago is the way computers are integrated into our homes. Even those who don't work from home usually have a corner dedicated to a computer – an essential tool for research and communication. The home office is the norm, rather than the exception.

As with televisions, computers are often beautifully designed these days, so why camouflage them? In addition, they are such an important part of our everyday life that they need to be located somewhere convenient. I would avoid putting them in a bedroom – an area within the living room or kitchen is far more practical.

All you need to create a workable home office is a suitable table, comfortable chair and appropriate storage for paper and the like, plus – and this is essential – enough wall and floor sockets, to avoid dangerous trailing wires. Well-considered lighting is also important. If you are disciplined, it should not be necessary to screen off the home office from the rest of your home.

ABOVE RIGHT The window alcove of a living room provides the location for this compact home office, which benefits from the view outside. The light above reflects the shape of the desk and helps to separate it from the rest of the room.

RIGHT This built-in computer area fits snugly into one end of a children's bedroom. Cupboards provide useful storage space for CDs, DVDs and accompanying paraphernalia, while also concealing trailing wires and electrical plugs.

FAR RIGHT This pull-out cupboard door holds an ingenious surprise: it is in fact a seat on wheels, designed to be used with a shelf that also doubles as a desk. When not needed, it is simply pushed back in and out of sight.

THIS PAGE *This understated study area has been incorporated into a corridor space. Floating shelves display books, photographs, glass vases by Anna Torfs and a metal sculpture by Megaron against the textured backdrop of ribbed plaster. The black trestle table by B & B Italia echoes the lines of the shelves.*

Cooking and eating

No longer just a place in which to cook (thankfully), the contemporary kitchen should be designed as the pivotal room within the house.

The kitchen is today so much more than a kitchen. It is often the main family living space, an informal dining room and a home office or play area. Walk into any kitchen showroom and that becomes apparent – designers no longer put together a row of cupboards for storage with a work surface and sink. The boundaries have become increasingly blurred, so much so that ranges are also likely to include options for seating, dining, working and so forth.

The place to start, therefore, is you and your family. Write a list itemizing what you need from your kitchen, in terms of living as well as cooking. Be realistic: a new kitchen will not magically turn you into someone who loves producing a five-course gourmet meal. Don't clutter it with expensive gadgets you barely know how to use. If your idea of entertaining is to get the caterers in, then admit it. As with all of your home, the aim is to achieve a space that works for you, not for the person you imagine you would like to be.

If, however, you do love to cook, then think about what kind of dishes you most like to make, which equipment you have to find space for and what else is needed to make preparation easier. The way a Japanese kitchen is designed is very different from an American one, for example. Experienced kitchen designers are worth their weight in gold, because they will be able to create something for you that will make your life run so effortlessly you will simply not know how you managed before. That is why I am not going to attempt to tell you how to design a kitchen yourself; it is a job I tender out to specialists myself and my advice would be to do your research and find a professional designer who truly understands what you want from this most important of rooms.

What most of us require from the kitchen is a relaxing place, where we can chat to friends or spend time with family. The kitchen should, therefore, be in the biggest space you can create – not

OPPOSITE *The opaque glass used for this striking worktop is lit from beneath, creating a sense of drama within the kitchen. Tall dark wood cupboards emphasize the grid-like design of strong vertical and horizontal lines.*

ABOVE *Traditional with a modern twist, this is very much a cook's kitchen. The solid Carrera marble work surface is both beautiful and functional, its glossy surface highlighted by the line of glass bowls from Kelly Hoppen Store.*

RIGHT *Hanging lights over the dining table is an effective way of marking out the eating area from the rest of the room in an open-plan space. Here two horn pendants from Ochre create a focal point over the dark wood of the table surface.*

ABOVE *In a purpose-built apartment that already had a newly fitted kitchen, the cupboard carcasses have been retained, but the doors replaced in order to give a different look. The circular table and curved chairs from Modénature, with light by Kevin Reilly above, contrast with its linear character.*

KELLY SAYS

I learnt at an early age that eating is not just about food. It is about creating a mood through tableware and accessories, setting the scene to share with friends.

MAKING THE MOST OF YOUR KITCHEN

Write down all the functions of the kitchen, including those of any adjoining living and dining spaces.

Think about who is going to use it, for what and at which times of the day.

Consider the type of cooking you want to do and which equipment you need.

Be disciplined about not cluttering it with items you are unlikely to use.

Ensure you have lighting that is both practical and atmospheric, according to the occasion.

Make sure you have adequate storage for every type of item.

Think about the way you live and how you like to entertain.

Remember that you need a space that not only looks great, but that is easy to maintain.

OPPOSITE BOTTOM *The dining area in a kitchen/family living space has been kept very simple with all-white furniture and a pendant light that echoes the shape of the table. The use of white has the effect of visually separating this zone from the rest of the room. The artwork is by Arman.*

ABOVE RIGHT *Dining need not be restricted by convention. This intimate area has been created within a master bedroom, perfect for breakfast. Furniture is antique, other than the two upholstered chairs.*

RIGHT *In a custom-built wine cellar with space for dining, a fabric made of cork makes a witty reference to the surroundings. The rug, screen and table are antique Chinese; the room divider is of perforated bronze.*

surprisingly, it is the part of the house most likely to be extended or knocked through. As it will almost certainly be planned around a series of zones, it is crucial to make sure these work together well. If you want to take control of this part of the design process, it is absolutely essential that you work to proper scaled drawings. If you are not mathematical, then employ someone else to do it for you; it is simply too important to risk getting wrong. You really do need to know the size of sofa, table or computer desk you can fit in and how much room there will be for people to walk around each zone. One-space living is the contemporary way to live, but achieving it demands a clear head and a methodical approach.

Lighting can be used to demarcate each zone, be it providing acute task lighting for a chopping surface or a soft glow over a dining table. You could even install a control panel, which will alter light settings within a room at the touch of a keypad.

There may still be times, however, when you want to embrace more formal dining. It seems a shame that many people today have sacrificed their dining room for a family snug or home office. In my view, there is much to be said for formal dining as well as the informal type. Whether it is Sunday lunch with the family, a dinner party for clients or a religious festival, nothing can create atmosphere so much as a room dedicated to eating well. There is a wonderful sense of occasion about taking the best glassware, plates or cutlery and laying the table in a truly special way.

When it comes to furniture, comfortable chairs are an absolute must. After all, the best meals are those that drift on from lunch into the afternoon, or dinner well into the night. That is never going to happen if backs and bottoms start to ache. Just as you need to try out sofas and beds before buying, the same is true of dining chairs. When it comes to style, remember that you can create a new look by re-covering them in different materials – even choosing one fabric for the seats and another for the backs. You don't have to have each chair matching, either – in my own home I have used two enormous carvers in faux crocodile as a contrast of scale and texture with white leather dining chairs.

If you are fortunate enough to have a dining room, then decorate it in such a way as to generate a sense of wonder. This is the place to hang your best paintings or display your most treasured objects – not in order to show off, but to leave guests feeling that they have enjoyed a very special time with you.

ABOVE *A table coated in textured plaster mixed with marble dust and mother-of-pearl natural pigment is the centrepiece of this monochromatic scheme. Glass doors along one wall pivot open into the hall when a bigger dining space is required and also allow views through to the sculptural staircase. The dark glass vase beneath the Davide Medri mirror is by Amanda Brisbane; the other glassware is by Anna Torfs.*

LEFT *The family dining room of an original Arts & Crafts house has been rejuvenated with a calm neutral scheme and contemporary furniture, including 'Velin' chairs by Christian Liaigre. Hanging three identical pendant lights above the dining table is a modern alternative to using a traditional chandelier.*

OPPOSITE *In today's world true luxury is often quietly understated. This close-up shows a hand-crafted Linley dining table made of ebony with superb mother-of-pearl detailing.*

Waking up and winding down

The bedroom is central to your wellbeing and comfort, so spend time creating one that reflects you and makes you happy.

It is common sense that the place where you wake up in the morning and fall asleep at night will have a profound effect on your general wellbeing. If this doesn't feel right, how will anything feel right? Your bedroom is your nest, a comfort zone, a microcosm of the rest of your world. Forget other people – this is a place that is all about you.

If you have space for a separate dressing room or closet, I heartily recommend you make the most of it. Apart from the sheer luxury of having somewhere spacious to store clothes, the real joy is in having a bedroom that need never feel cluttered or untidy. Now is the time to decide on your priorities for this most special of spaces,

OPPOSITE *A sumptuous padded and upholstered bedhead has been positioned behind the existing leather one of this double bed, making it look much grander. Pale horizontal runners on cushions, bedspread and curtains make the room appear bigger. The adjustable reading lights are by India Mahdavi.*

ABOVE *This wall of dark wood shutters allows light to filter into the room from the windows behind, but at night it is lit to dramatic effect by cylindrical glass pendants from Solzi Luce. It creates a strong textural statement against which the softness of fabric and flooring plays.*

RIGHT *Instead of using conventional table or wall lamps, a pair of large white metal pendants seem to float over the bedside tables. Velvets and linens in whites and off-whites combine to impart a feeling of rest and sanctuary.*

BELOW *Symmetry and balance are key in this calming bedroom. The arrangement of six cushions, from large at the back to small in the front, and the runner down the bedspread are classic Kelly Hoppen in style.*

BOTTOM LEFT *A triple-width bunk bed is a fun addition to the children's bedroom in this family holiday chalet, stained black to contrast*

with the taupe of the beams on the ceiling. The bunk bed, complete with generous storage below, is a functional choice.

BOTTOM RIGHT *Black floating shelves are a chic alternative to the conventional bedside table. The top one is, in fact, a drawer, as well as being a useful surface. Wall lights, such as this one by Isometrix, are a practical bedside solution.*

MAKING THE MOST OF YOUR BEDROOM

This is a room that is all about you, so write a list itemizing what you most want from it.

Clutter is a stress factor, so make sure you have enough storage for your clothes, shoes and so on.

Comfort is also a priority, so this means having the most wonderful bed you can afford.

Splash out on the best bedlinen, too. You will never regret the extra cost.

Find a way of dressing the bed that will make your heart lift whenever you walk into the room.

Think both about natural light to wake up by and how to light the room at night for atmosphere.

Surround yourself with objects and pictures that you truly love.

Make sure the room smells great.

be it a good bedside lamp for reading by or a television to watch when you want to laze in bed. Bedrooms often double up as home gyms or offices. Personally, I would resist the idea – how can you really enjoy your bedroom if you are surrounded by equipment that makes you feel guilty? If there is no option, then invest in a screen to hide the offending objects from view.

Of course, it may be that you are designing a bedroom for someone else to use, such as a child or a guest. Children love to help with designs for their own bedrooms – and why not? It is really fun to remember how inventive and creative you were as a child, so listen to what they say and at least try to meet them halfway. Guest rooms are often an afterthought –

the place for the not-so-good bed or unadventurous art. I would say, go to the other extreme. Create a guest room full of special touches, so the memory of it lingers with your visitors and makes them feel happy whenever they think about you.

Naturally enough, in the bedroom it is the bed that is the dominant feature. Choose one for comfort above all else – and that does mean going out and trying them – and then look for ways of dressing it for maximum effect. Tall headboards are both supportive to lean back on and make a strong visual statement. If you want a glamorous finish, such as ostrich or suede, then faux varieties are more practical because they are easier to clean. You must also buy the best bedding you can afford, not only for yourself but for guests. It is so gratifying when a visitor comments on how well they slept and how much they appreciated the softness of the linen or towels. Good bedlinen is an absolute must. Linen sheets feel fantastic, but these days there are also excellent ranges of pure cotton. Whether you prefer duvets or blankets is a personal choice, but the same rule still applies: buy the very best you can afford and have them cleaned regularly. I love to use sexy, sumptuous bedspreads in wonderful touchy-feely fabrics – in my view, bedrooms should be unashamedly sexy.

ABOVE *In my own bedroom, I layered up dress fabrics, such as the gorgeous velvet used for the sumptuous bedspread, rather than ones recommended for domestic use. Texture is the driving force in the room, from the white leather headboard to the shag-pile carpet.*

LEFT *In a teenager's bedroom wallpaper that resembles Post-It notes has been used for a witty and individual touch. High shelves above the bed are ideal for storing treasured and personal objects.*

Bedrooms should be all about pleasing the senses, which is why I often choose thick, luxurious carpet for this room, even when I am using mainly wood or stone elsewhere. Windows need careful thought as well: are you the sort of person who likes to wake up to light or do you prefer it blacked out until you surface? I fall into the former camp, so have only the lightest parachute silk at my windows. If you are not a morning person, you might want to consider having blackout blinds or shutters installed, softened with a layer of dress curtains.

Lastly, because your bedroom is about you, surround yourself with treasures that make you feel happy – whether these are family photographs or favourite books.

ABOVE *The deep purple of the crushed-velvet headboard and cushions on Christian Liaigre's 'Ré' bed provides an accent of colour, reinforced by the 'Sud' bench, also by Christian Liaigre, the bedside stool and the glass lamp base.*

OPPOSITE *Four-poster beds are natural star pieces and this one has been upholstered in pale blue silk. Cushions arranged at the top and bottom emphasize its oriental quality, along with the 'Lanterne' lamps by Christian Liaigre.*

KELLY SAYS

Always find time to make the bed properly. It takes only five minutes, but gives you such a lift when you walk into the bedroom at the end of a long and tiring day.

Bathing and indulging

Whether you prefer taking a leisurely bath or an exhilarating shower, your bathroom should make you feel cosseted.

THIS PAGE *In my own bathroom a black runner of wood stained to a wenge finish leads to the elegantly shaped Agape bathtub with taps from my own range for Waterfront, set against chiselled marble walls. The low Japanese-style bench and single white marble step emphasize its Zen-like beauty. The white stool and metal side table are both by India Mahdavi.*

OPPOSITE *At the other end of the bathroom I opted for a spacious walk-in shower, with clear glass doors complementing the marble walls. As before, the fittings are my own design for Waterfront. The dark wood floor grounds the scheme and is illuminated by low-level floor washers that enhance its texture and density.*

OPPOSITE TOP *Original shoji panels in linden wood stained black set the scene for this Japanese-style bathing temple, with its black slate bath and old stone floor. Fabric blinds complement the look superbly.*

OPPOSITE BOTTOM LEFT *Pure and simple are the key words in this en-suite bathroom. The classic design of the freestanding bath fits perfectly with the tongue-and-groove walls and dark stained reclaimed floorboards.*

OPPOSITE BOTTOM RIGHT *Marble is a versatile stone that comes in many colours and finishes. In this contemporary bathroom one with rich veining has been used, becoming the dominant decorative feature of the room.*

BELOW *Baths and basins are now available in really sculptural shapes, so you can create interesting vistas with sanitaryware alone. These twin basins have an almost abstract effect against a panel of taupe wood.*

BELOW RIGHT *If you are fortunate enough to have a bathroom with a view, then make the most of it by situating the bathtub close to the window. Here external plantation shutters provide privacy when necessary.*

I am always amazed when I hear people say that today's bathrooms are more like home spas. As far as I am concerned, they are much more than that. In fact, spas can be my idea of design torture with their dripping water, rolled towels and floating orchids. All that strikes me as far too gimmicky. I love bathrooms that are more like temples – luxurious spaces of cool stone and ultra-soft lighting. Total calm – a neutral space.

As with all design, you first have to decide on your own priorities for the space. I like to shower, but I really love to bathe, so for me the bath will always be the central focus of the room. In many ways, bathrooms are actually quite easy to design, because they are essentially a grid system. I use either two contrasting types of stone – perhaps one polished and one honed – or one stone combined with a wood, in order to create vertical and horizontal panels against which the bathroom appliances are set. Stone is now widely available at very affordable prices, so having pieces custom-cut for you is no longer the domain of the super-rich. You do have to make sure your floor joists are strong enough to support it, though. If in doubt, you could use stone tiles instead.

Stone is the natural core material of a bathroom, because it mixes well with other hard materials such as glass or wood. It is also the ideal companion to underfloor heating, because it radiates heat rather than absorbing it, as wood does. In fact, everything seems to be readily available in stone today, from shower enclosures and bath surrounds to cistern panels and basins. If buying the latter, square chunky shapes look far more modern than the domed ceramic styles of the previous decade. Never skimp on taps – they are like jewellery setting off the perfect outfit.

En-suite bathrooms are often created from space commandeered from other rooms, so it is not unusual for them to have no natural light. That means the artificial lighting you install is even more important than in other rooms. Bathroom lighting needs careful consideration on many levels: you will need task lighting for activities such as shaving or applying make-up, as well as fabulously atmospheric lighting for when you just want to lie in the tub and forget the cares of the day. Avoid having light directed straight down onto your head near a vanity mirror, as it will cast you into your own shadow. Uplighting is preferable because it will bounce light up onto the ceiling, bleaching out

shadows and making you look wonderful. The best type of lighting for applying make-up is provided by vertical light fittings placed on each side of the mirror, as in the days of old Hollywood. Be cautious about buying vanity units with integral lights, however, as these are often fluorescent, which is not always flattering to certain skin tones.

A room that is for destressing, as much as for the functional business of washing, needs to be kept tidy, so include plenty of storage for essential items such as beauty products, towels and loo rolls at the design stage. Storage of small-scale objects, such as cotton-wool balls or hair grips, is also important in the bathroom. You don't have to commission customized storage solutions – it is simply a question of sourcing suitable containers that are in scale with each item; there is plenty of choice in high street shops.

What matters in the bathroom is that you create a sanctuary where you can leave your worries at the door and come out feeling revived and rejuvenated. The most expensive bath oil in the world can't achieve that unless the bathroom itself makes you feel relaxed and refreshed. This is your most personal space, so design it for you.

BELOW *Bathrooms should be a direct reflection of your own taste and personality. Here tongue-and-groove panels used horizontally add a contemporary twist to a dark-toned masculine bathroom. Alabaster lights set above a beaten-silver basin bring out texture and depth.*

OPPOSITE *A vanity unit constructed from Venetian mirror is the centrepiece in this compact but elegant guest bathroom. Feathered paper sandwiched between panels of glass creates a softly textured wall between this and the adjacent dressing room.*

MAKING THE MOST OF YOUR BATHROOM

Think of your bathroom as a temple – make it as luxurious as possible.

Decide whether the bath or shower should take priority.

Never skimp on fittings such as taps or towel rails – you should always buy the best you can afford.

Stone is the natural material for bathrooms – even if you can't afford it throughout, you should aim to introduce it where possible.

Underfloor heating is an asset in the bathroom, particularly if you have a stone floor.

Good lighting is essential – you want to look as beautiful as possible in your own bathroom.

Mirrors are necessary, but don't install floor-to-ceiling ones unless you have no hang-ups.

Well-thought-out storage is essential, for both bulky goods, such as spare loo rolls, and small ones, such as cotton-wool balls.

PRIVATE MOMENTS
Cloakrooms are too often much-ignored rooms, but in my opinion they should be given the same care and consideration as bathrooms. While on one level they have a practical purpose – you might use yours to store coats as well as to house a guest loo, for example – like the hall, they are all about presenting your signature to visitors. A cloakroom should make a guest feel welcome, so it should be lit sympathetically and have plenty of clean towels and soap. However, it is also a chance to create a note of drama: small rooms are often the best in which to sound a theatrical ring, because the cost is relatively inexpensive and the result can be sensational.

Think first about the materials you are going to use. Cloakrooms are the ideal place for strong statement pieces in wood or stone. Do not, however, be tempted to buy something because it is 'gimmicky' or 'fun'. People are sometimes tempted to use the cloakroom as their bad-taste corner, a spot for keeping vulgar literature or embarrassing photographs. I think they should be places that make a visitor say 'wow' in admiration, rather than try to entertain them in a facile way.

Once you have selected a basin – the centrepiece of this small room – introduce textural contrast on the walls and floor. As in a hall, I might create a runner of stone on a wood floor, or vice versa. It is a witty touch, almost like a landing strip guiding the visitor to the loo. The cloakroom is a great place to experiment with touches such as this, because if you don't achieve the look you envisaged, you won't have spent a fortune. In fact, if you want to try out the skills of a professional for laying floors, applying a specialist plaster finish or constructing cabinetry, the cloakroom is an excellent place in which to begin.

I also like to scale everything up in a small space, perhaps by introducing a vast mirror over the sink or hanging a decadent chandelier. Catching the eye and drawing it upwards makes a small room appear larger. I like visitors to smile when they visit this 'smallest room' and appreciate the thought that has gone into creating something unexpected and exciting.

KELLY SAYS
Every part of a home is of equal importance, so don't skimp when it comes to hidden corners.

OPPOSITE *In a guest loo the focal point is likely to be the basin. Within the curved walls of this cloakroom, a piece of marble has been sliced to fit the space exactly, with a glamorously illuminated mirror above emphasizing its proportions.*

RIGHT *For my own cloakroom, I designed a pattern for the walls on the computer and had it made up in plaster. My signature runner is here translated into smoky glass, which infuses the whole space with a seductive sultry atmosphere.*

BELOW LEFT *The beauty of designing a cloakroom is that it is not necessary for the basin and loo to match. Here a chunk of wood has been carved into a fabulously tactile basin that seems to float against the black tiled walls.*

BELOW CENTRE *Scala blue limestone has been carved into a luxurious vanity top, in which the rectangular basin is set. The graphic line of the tap complements this architectural look perfectly.*

BELOW RIGHT *A slab of Carrera marble has been carved into a double basin set on a dark wood vanity unit. Spacing the taps so far apart accentuates the generous dimensions of this elegant design.*

Taking it outside

Whether you have a landscaped garden or a city roof terrace, you need to consider your outside space in tandem with your inside one.

It used to be the case that houses were most often designed in isolation from their surroundings. One person took responsibility for the garden, another for the interior. Today it is unusual for the two areas to be considered so separately from one another. Increasingly there is a trend – particularly in modern architect-built houses – for there to be more of an inside-outside approach, with each respectfully reflecting the other.

In recent years we have also been enjoying a new love affair with light. Nothing seems to excite the spirit more than a big open expanse of blue sky. Privacy is important in some locations, particularly in densely populated urban ones, but interestingly many people are forgoing that in favour of keeping their windows uncovered and allowing natural light to pour into their homes. My own home looks out on a cityscape of cars, trains and planes – it wouldn't be everyone's choice, but I absolutely love it and have no desire to screen it out.

The fact is that if you have any external space at all, whether it is acres of garden or a compact roof terrace, it makes no sense to give it a different design signature from the house. The garden designers I work with express the ethos I bring to a home, usually

ABOVE *Sixteen huge sculptural pots of topiary set the signature look for my own eco-built urban roof terrace. Furniture is a mix of pieces I relocated from inside to outside and contemporary garden designs.*

OPPOSITE *A sculptural screen of glass bricks is an inspired way of partitioning off a barbecue area from the rest of the garden. Light and water combine to make it appear as if it is continually shimmering and moving.*

by imposing quite a rigid structure through a grid system and then allowing the edges to blur. In the gardens I oversee, flowers are not as important as the form, texture and scale of plants and trees – those same three words are a continual undercurrent in my interior designs.

It is also important to bring comfort to the outdoors. Choose furniture that has the same luxury feel that you might have found on an old-fashioned ocean liner, with deep cushions and adjustable chair backs. Buy tables that are large enough to seat many friends, so you can throw informal supper parties when the weather allows. And, most importantly, remember that your outdoor space will benefit from well-thought-out lighting. A few spike spotlights uplighting selected trees can make an incredible difference. However, just as you would in a room, you must keep the effect balanced. All trees and shrubs look wonderful when lit, but don't overdo it – less is more, as with so much in life.

You must also think about maintenance. Plants do need regular watering in order to survive – if you are too busy to remember, then it is essential to install an automated irrigation system. If you don't know the nature of particular plants, then do seek professional advice from a gardener. Shade lovers won't thrive in direct sunlight; sun worshippers won't appreciate a shady corner. A little understanding can make all the difference.

In areas that connect directly with the house, you can underline the link between internal and external by repeating materials. For example, you might run the same stone from the living room or kitchen to a terrace, making a strong visual tie between the two. Remember that it is not just a question of being inside a house and looking out, but of being outside and looking in. There are views and vistas in each direction – the trick is to find ways of complementing both. Lighting can be key: there is something very comforting about looking in on welcoming lit rooms from the dark.

OPPOSITE *In this contemporary architect-built house with huge windows on all sides, it was essential that the garden reflected its character. A sea of tall grasses lead the eye to the trees beyond.*

ABOVE *Perfect for locations where the climate permits, upholstered external seating, such as this generous modular design, strikes the right note of luxury and relaxation against a backdrop of tropical trees.*

MAKING THE MOST OF YOUR GARDEN

Any outside space needs to be considered as an extension of the house.

Think about both the views from inside out and those from outside in.

Look for ways of linking the two areas through materials or accents of colour.

Remember that although you may not be able to actually sit in your outside space throughout the year, it can still be designed with a view to providing year-round visual interest.

External lighting means that you can extend the views from day into night in both summer and winter.

Choose garden furniture that is as comfortable as your living-room seating.

Remember that foliage lasts longer than flowers, so you need plants with textural interest and architectural form.

If you are not a dedicated gardener, it is essential to have a built-in irrigation system to keep the plants alive.

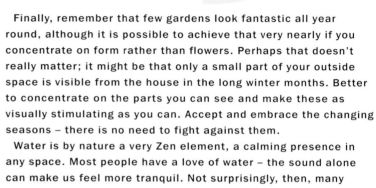

KELLY SAYS
Gardens are exterior rooms that should reflect the shape, scale and texture of surrounding buildings.

Finally, remember that few gardens look fantastic all year round, although it is possible to achieve that very nearly if you concentrate on form rather than flowers. Perhaps that doesn't really matter; it might be that only a small part of your outside space is visible from the house in the long winter months. Better to concentrate on the parts you can see and make these as visually stimulating as you can. Accept and embrace the changing seasons – there is no need to fight against them.

Water is by nature a very Zen element, a calming presence in any space. Most people have a love of water – the sound alone can make us feel more tranquil. Not surprisingly, then, many people desire ways of integrating it into the home, usually by connecting the interior to the exterior, such as having doors that open onto water features or pools. However, where swimming pools are concerned, this cuts both ways. Rather than being purely functional in design, swimming pool areas are now likely to mirror the style of the home through furniture, lighting and general ambience. It is all about creating a sense of comfort and intimacy, both inside and outside.

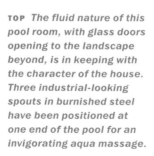

TOP *The fluid nature of this pool room, with glass doors opening to the landscape beyond, is in keeping with the character of the house. Three industrial-looking spouts in burnished steel have been positioned at one end of the pool for an invigorating aqua massage.*

CENTRE *This is another view of the pool room shown above. The modern circular upholstered seating is echoed in form by the bronze sculpture by Amanda Brisbane that is set into the brick wall.*

LEFT *The strong moulded shape of these black plastic pool-side loungers makes for a stark contrast of dark and light beside this outdoor pool. Leaving the chairs cushionless accentuates their bold form.*

OPPOSITE TOP *This luxurious lap pool has been elevated to a design statement with decorative chandeliers hung from the ceiling above the water and bordered linen curtains at the French windows. At the far end is a living area (see bottom right).*

OPPOSITE BOTTOM LEFT *Another view of the same room looking in at the pool from outside, showing how the windows open up to allow light to flood in. Swimmers can enjoy the view of the surrounding landscaped gardens from inside.*

OPPOSITE BOTTOM RIGHT *This comfortable living area with fireplace, seating and equestrian art is, in fact, the living area of the pool shown above, with the Jacuzzi in the foreground. Doors open onto the garden beyond.*

The inside-outside house

THE CHALLENGE: To transform a beautifully designed architectural gem into a workable and comfortable family home. To instil it with character and warmth. **THE SOLUTION:** To celebrate the excellent proportions of the space, while finding ways to visually link the suite of rooms, so that one signature runs throughout.

In this house my involvement began at a fairly late stage. It was built by the architect Terry Farrell, who did a sensational job ensuring the interior was flooded with natural light. The brief my clients gave me was to turn it from an amazing house into a home that was more personal to them, while still being sympathetic to the extraordinary qualities inherent in the architecture.

I love natural light myself and was captivated by the way the house and garden have been so well integrated, but there is a danger that such

KEY CONSIDERATIONS

Taking an architectural show-stopper and turning it into a welcoming family home.

Celebrating and making the most of the generous amounts of natural light.

Solving practical problems, such as how to stop the dog from escaping.

Accentuating the inherent architectural beauty of the space, in particular the use of natural light.

Making the most of the space in the long gallery-style hallway.

Creating a sense of flow from room to room.

Giving each room a sense of identity.

Ensuring that the garden feels visually linked to the house.

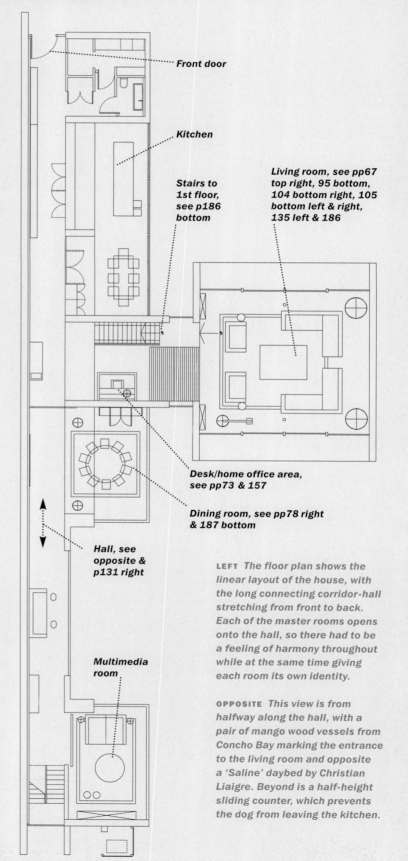

Front door

Kitchen

Stairs to 1st floor, see p186 bottom

Living room, see pp67 top right, 95 bottom, 104 bottom right, 105 bottom left & right, 135 left & 186

Desk/home office area, see pp73 & 157

Dining room, see pp78 right & 187 bottom

Hall, see opposite & p131 right

Multimedia room

LEFT *The floor plan shows the linear layout of the house, with the long connecting corridor-hall stretching from front to back. Each of the master rooms opens onto the hall, so there had to be a feeling of harmony throughout while at the same time giving each room its own identity.*

OPPOSITE *This view is from halfway along the hall, with a pair of mango wood vessels from Concho Bay marking the entrance to the living room and opposite a 'Saline' daybed by Christian Liaigre. Beyond is a half-height sliding counter, which prevents the dog from leaving the kitchen.*

ABOVE The low narrow window above the fireplace in the living room looks out onto the garden, emphasizing the house's relationship with its exterior. The artwork above is by Peter Beard. An unusual arrangement of two L-shaped sofas opposite each other has been used to provide symmetry and create a feeling of intimacy around the fire.

LEFT Looking from the living room to the hall and stairs that lead to the upper level of the house. One of the additions I made to this room were the floor-to-ceiling bookcases, which bring a feeling of warmth to the room because they can be used to display favourite objects. The dark wood of these and the coffee table also acts as a foil to the pale stone used throughout the house. The floor lamp in front of the bookcase is by India Mahdavi.

OPPOSITE BOTTOM The formal dining room has floor-to-ceiling windows on two sides, so the round table had to be placed centrally, acting as a pivotal point within the room. The chairs are upholstered in a combination of leather on the seats and linen on the backs, while a specialist plaster finish underlines the textural contrast. A 'Merlot' floor lamp by Christian Liaigre has been chosen instead of an overhead light.

a modern space can tend to feel a little cold and impersonal. When I saw the hall – a great long gallery-like space – it seemed obvious to break this up with well-chosen pieces of furniture, objects and art that would hold the eye and inject a sense of the clients' personality, without detracting from the brilliance of the design. There were also practical problems to solve, such as how to contain the owners' boisterous dog. My solution was to install a half-height counter between the hall and kitchen that could be slid closed when needed (see page 185). It serves its purpose brilliantly without conflicting with the ambience of the house.

As a material, stone can also be cold, so I chose key pieces of furniture in dark woods, such as the imposing bookcases in the living room. Wood is a good foil to stone, because it introduces a sense of warmth. In this case it also strengthened the link between the interior and the surrounding garden.

The ground floor of the house is, in effect, a suite of rooms that each opens onto the hall. So it was important to come up with a design scheme that both achieved a visual flow from one room to the next, and also imprinted each space with its own character and look.

Naturally, the views onto the garden were a big consideration in a house with such huge windows running around the walls. The planting is mainly architectural, with strong shapes of textured foliage that can be enjoyed all year round. This needs to be well maintained, so that it never blocks out the natural light the house enjoys.

ABOVE *The view from the gallery upstairs looking down onto the hall below. I used furniture, such as the low bench, to break up the expanse of stone. It is also a practical place on which to display vases of flowers and other objects. Skylights let light flood into the house at all times of the year.*

Index

ACKNOWLEDGEMENTS

I would like to thank all my clients who have allowed me back into their homes to photograph the finished results. Without them, the book would not have been possible.

A big thank you also to:

My Interior Design team, who execute every job with such precision. You are all extraordinary. Olivia Lewzey, who keeps me breathing on a daily basis. John Carter for your love and care of all these homes. Rica for your continuous help and care. I cannot imagine life without you. Jacqui Small for your professionalism and support. Helen Chislett for once again interpreting my thoughts into words. Vincent Knapp for your extraordinary vision through the lens – you are a master. Lawrence Morton for your creative design, and Zia Mattocks for editing the book with such care and patience. Melanie Lanick for your care and support throughout this book. You have been a pillar of strength and calm. Michael Lindsay – Watson and Alexandra Bennaim for everything again and again. Christina Ojo for your amazing work on the sample boards. Rob Clift for making lighting such fun. Sofia Stainton for sharing your wisdom and talent. Clark Gallagher and your team for your hard work and patience on site. Luciano Giubbilei for designing extraordinary gardens. Dorean Scott – once again, you are a magician when it comes to fabric. Randle Siddeley for your extraordinary team and craftsmen when creating outdoor spaces. Jazz and Tara for being the most organized and creative children I have worked with. Rita, Maria and Fernando for taking such good care of us during the photo shoots. And last but not least, thank you Marianne and Brian – I really value your skill and talent.

Architects whose work is featured in this book:

TERRY FARRELL AND PARTNERS
7 Hatton Street
London NW8 8PL
UK
Tel: +44 (0)20 7258 3433
www.terryfarrell.co.uk

SHLOMIT FRENKEL
70 Heh B'Iyar Street
61298 Tel Aviv
Israel
frenkelarch@bezeqint.net

BERNHARD LERJEN
Untere Mattenstrasse
9 3920 Zermatt
Switzerland

KAREN MAZE
Kelly Hoppen Interiors
2 Munden Street
London W14 0RH
UK
Tel: +44 (0)20 7471 3350
www.kellyhoppen.com

MUNKENBECK & MARSHALL
ARCHITECTS
135 Curtain Road
London EC2A 3BX
UK
Tel: +44 (0)20 7739 3300
www.mandm.uk.com

REBECCA RASMUSSEN ARCHITECT PC
140 West 83rd Street ~1
New York, NY 10024
USA
Tel: +1 212 362 9546

Additional credits

Author portrait, page 6: photography by Nick Haddow (www.nickhaddow.com).
Artwork featured, pages 22–3: © Flip Schulke.
Artwork features, pages 30–1, 68–9 and 126–7: Vanessa Beecroft, VB51.001.NT, VB51 Schloss, Vinseback, Steiheim; photo by Nic Tenwiggenhorn; © 2002 Vanessa Beecroft.
Artwork featured, page 132 left: Valerie Belin, (Untitled) Mirror Series (1997), silver gelatin print, 100 x 80cm; © Valerie Belin.
Artwork featured, pages 140–1: Hans Op De Beeck, Determination (13) (boy) and Determination (2) (girl), lightboxes; courtesy of the artist and Galerie Ron Mandos, Amsterdam.

THE PART OF
Y BEEN LO
MING
TH

OPPOSITE PAGE: A close-up of the dining room shown previously
this blends with the banner-style runners hung along the wa
creates an atmosphere that is truly inviting.
BELOW LEFT: The classic lines of this Mies van der Rohe stool
an interesting contrast to the curved stainless steel legs a